PASTOR, OUR MARRIAGE
IS IN TROUBLE

PASTOR, OUR MARRIAGE IS IN TROUBLE

A GUIDE TO *SHORT-TERM COUNSELING*

CHARLES L. RASSIEUR

THE WESTMINSTER PRESS
PHILADELPHIA

© 1988 Charles L. Rassieur

All rights reserved—With the exception of the Pastoral Marriage Counseling Questionnaire following chapter 5, no part of this book may be reproduced in any form without permission in writing from the publisher, except by a reviewer who wishes to quote brief passages in connection with a review in magazine or newspaper.

Scripture quotations are from the Revised Standard Version of the Bible, copyrighted 1946, 1952, © 1971, 1973 by the Division of Christian Education of the National Council of the Churches of Christ in the U.S.A., and are used by permission.

Book design by Gene Harris

First edition

Published by The Westminster Press®
Philadelphia, Pennsylvania

PRINTED IN THE UNITED STATES OF AMERICA

9 8 7 6 5 4 3 2 1

Library of Congress Cataloging-in-Publication Data

Rassieur, Charles L., 1938–
  Pastor, our marriage is in trouble.

  Bibliography: p.
  1. Marriage counseling.   2. Pastoral counseling.
I. Title.
BV4012.27.R37   1988   253.5   88-5600
ISBN 0-664-25033-5 (pbk.)

Dedicated

to the countless married couples

who have trusted me to be their counselor

and to hear their mutual pain

as well as their shared hopes

for the future of their marriage

CONTENTS

PREFACE

The problems and the complexities of a painful marital relationship can be quite overwhelming for any counselor, and especially for the parish pastor for whom marriage counseling is not a specialty but a necessity among many other pastoral responsibilities. The purpose of this book is to meet the need felt by many pastors, regardless of their years of experience, for reliable guidance in pastoral marriage counseling.

The following five assumptions have guided my preparation of this book:

1. Short-term marital intervention is the normative and appropriate model for parish pastors.

2. Although some clergy may have had one quarter of Clinical Pastoral Education in seminary and some personal counseling for themselves, most are not equipped—nor do they envision themselves—as sophisticated marriage therapists.

3. The pastor holds a unique position and office in the church, which offers both the authority and the opportunity to intervene and bring healing to many conflicted marriages.

4. Not all marriage conflicts can be resolved, no matter how skilled the counselor or therapist.

5. The pastor as counselor is inevitably involved in evaluation and often the referral of troubled couples, regardless of how sophisticated that assessment is.

A structured short-term counseling approach is presented here as the normative model for pastoral intervention in marital crises. A model is just that; it is not intended to be an inviolable rule. The criticism for any model is that it appears to offer a simplistic approach to a complex process. In fact, I have written this book fully persuaded that marital conflict holds many complicated dynamics. For just that reason, the purpose of the short-term marriage counseling model presented in the following chapters is to offer the best opportunity for the unique resources of pastoral counseling to make a constructive and promising intervention.

Some readers may turn to this book hoping to find new counseling methods that will quickly and effortlessly restore harmony to all troubled marriages. If that is a pastor's goal, there will be disappointment as the following pages are studied and put into practice. Although I will describe a variety of ways to work with couples in conflict, I am no longer persuaded that new techniques are the secret to increased success as a pastoral counselor. I am suspicious of gimmicks that are described by their proponents as being especially successful. Rather, I believe the heart of the counseling process, and the foundation for potential creative change in a troubled marriage, is the genuine care and concern of the pastor for each couple. Without the depth of quality of such a pastoral relationship, marriage counseling in the parish context will not hold much promise. But if that rich, caring pastoral relationship does exist, a transcending power for change can help a couple discover the reconciliation, joy, and love they are seeking.

This is intended to be a "how-to book" in the best sense of that phrase. Indeed, the idea for this book grew from the opportunities I have had for teaching workshops on marriage counseling to students at the Luther Northwestern Theological Seminary in St. Paul. As in those workshops, the intention in this book is to place in the hands of pastors and seminarians a tool that is usable and flexible and has potential for helping troubled marriages. Moreover, I offer this model for pastoral marriage counseling in the conviction that it is theologically and theoretically sound and that it allows for those using the model to adapt it easily to their own particular needs and counseling style.

In chapter 1 a rationale is developed for the need and opportunity for pastoral intervention in troubled marriages, as well as theological reflection for understanding marriage. Chapter 2 explains how the marriage counseling process begins with the initial pastoral contact with one or both spouses. The focus for chapter 3 is help for the pastor in preparing for individual counseling sessions with each spouse. Particular attention in chapter 3 is given to the Pastoral Marriage Counseling Questionnaire, which will be found at the end of the book. The final two sessions with the couple are reviewed in chapter 4, including a discussion of the pastor's options: either to recommend the ending of the counseling, to refer the couple to other professional resources, or to contract with them for further counseling sessions. The goal of chapter 5 is to examine important topics for marriage counseling, regardless of what approach or model is used by the counselor.

Here I wish to acknowledge my indebtedness to my friend William D. Tallevast, who many years ago introduced me to the Biographical

Marital Questionnaire published in Bernard L. Greene's book, *A Clinical Approach to Marital Problems: Evaluation and Management* (Springfield, Ill.: Charles C Thomas, 1970). Greene's questionnaire persuaded me of the many benefits of using this tool in the earliest stages of the marriage counseling process. The questionnaire presented in this book, while being influenced by many sources, was essentially created from my own clinical experiences and designed for the purposes of the parish pastor. Feel free to use it in your work.

At various stages of the development of this book I have been aware of the help I have received over the years both from colleagues with whom I have been associated as a pastoral counselor and the several professional consultants available to us. It would be a long list, and I would be afraid of leaving out someone's name. Needless to say, I owe a debt of thanks to all my associates who, through many discussions and case conferences, have greatly enriched my understanding of marriage and the practice of marriage counseling.

Six friends read all or part of the manuscript for this book before the final revision. I asked for their critical observations, while assuring them that I would be responsible for the final form. For their time and valuable suggestions, I gratefully acknowledge Frances D. Decker, Nils C. Friberg, Betsy L. Nagel, Eugene Orr, William A. Smith, and Donald R. White. My gratitude is extended also to my former employer, the Samaritan Counseling Center of Minneapolis/St. Paul, for study time during which I did much of my library research on marriage counseling.

I do not understand why my wife, Ginni, so readily supports my writing projects. But I am very thankful for her accommodations, as my time for writing has required considerable shifting in our shared domestic responsibilities. Now that this book on marriage is completed we are both looking forward to a more normal marital relationship for ourselves!

Please note that quotations from scripture are from the Revised Standard Version of the Bible. The quotation from Otto Piper in chapter 1 contains a reference to the King James Version.

New Brighton, Minnesota   C.L.R.

1

INTRODUCTION TO PASTORAL MARRIAGE COUNSELING

He answered, "Have you not read that he who made them from the beginning made them male and female, and said, 'For this reason a man shall leave his father and mother and be joined to his wife, and the two shall become one . . .' ? So they are no longer two but one . . . . What therefore God has joined together, let no man put asunder."

—Matthew 19:4–6

Mary Fordham often came into the church office during the week as she made preparations for the youth choir she directed. One day Pastor Elizabeth Boyd came out of her private office at the time that Mary was entering the church office, and they had a chance to exchange a few words. Immediately, Elizabeth sensed that something was troubling Mary very much. Because they were standing where others could hear their conversation, Elizabeth invited Mary into her own office.

As soon as the door was closed, Elizabeth said, "Mary, is something on your mind? Are you upset? You don't seem like yourself this morning." There was a long pause as Mary looked into her pastor's eyes for understanding. Then she started to cry.

"Yes, I'm very upset. Tom and I had another fight last night, and neither one of us got much sleep afterward. I didn't want to admit it to myself before, but now I must face it. Our marriage is really in trouble! We've tried everything we could think of over the last six months, but things have only gone from bad to worse!"

Most pastors can easily recall circumstances and conversations with parishioners similar to this one. The continuing mystery is that in God's wisdom a woman and a man, as different as they are, fulfill one of the fundamental laws of creation by choosing to be lifelong partners. And the continuing reality, despite illusions to the contrary created by the rituals and dances of courtship, is that marriage has more potential for conflict than any other relationship a person can enter. The irony is that the person we choose for our life's partner because he or she seems so ideal can become the source of the greatest hurt and pain we may ever experience. Perhaps Paul had reached a similar conclusion when, in the first century, he cautioned others with the observation that "those who marry will have worldly troubles, and I would spare you that" (1 Cor. 7:28b).

Unfortunately, the alarming rate of divorce today confirms Paul's recognition of the worldly troubles experienced by married persons. Although divorce statistics are not precise indicators of the health of contemporary marriage, researchers have found disturbing trends in the divorce rates of this century. In the nineteenth century, nearly every marriage ended by the death of one of the partners; divorce was quite rare. In this century, divorce rates began to rise in the mid-1940s, with a peak in 1979 and 1981. Sociologist Randall Collins has reached the discouraging conclusion that, based on the trends of the past decade, almost half of all new marriages in the coming years will end in divorce. And half of those divorced couples will have been married fewer than eight years.[1] However, the latest data reflect a recent decline in the national divorce rate of 4 percent between 1985 and 1986, bringing the rate to where it was in 1975.[2]

If divorce statistics have changed dramatically, so also have the currents and forces in society that affect the stability of marriages. Certainly, any accounting of the major influences on marriage today must include at least half a dozen new trends.

1. *The phenomenon of living together.* As recently as three decades ago a couple's cohabiting was referred to, rather disdainfully, as a common-law marriage. It was not respectable, and "nice people" did not do it! Now the young adult children of "nice people" quite commonly cohabit, or live together, as it is popularly called. One result of this recent change in accepted courting behaviors is that many young adults are postponing marriage. They have found a widely accepted means for intimacy and companionship without the obligations of a permanent commitment. Pastors will no doubt have increasing opportunities to do relationship counseling with such couples. For some pastors a special effort will be needed in order to set aside previous prejudices and offer sensitive pastoral care to couples who have chosen to delay making the traditional matrimonial commitments to each other.

2. *Young adults choosing career over marriage.* Not all young adults are living with a partner without the benefit of a wedding ceremony. But many young adults are delaying marriage because they want to continue their education or devote their energy to a promising career. Contraception and abortion have made sexual relations more common among young adults, and certainly marriage is not required for one to find partners for sexual expression. Many young adults prefer to become well established professionally and financially before making permanent commitments for marriage and family. Most pastors are seeing fewer couples marry before they are twenty, and an increasing number of couples are twenty-five or older before they are ready to commit themselves to marriage.

3. *Women returning to school and careers.* During World War II it was a necessity for women to leave home and go into the nation's factories. Fortunately we are not now at war, but for economic and personal reasons, fewer women are remaining at home. In fact, many couples feel it is a financial necessity for the wife to be a breadwinner also. An increasing number of women are either returning to college or moving directly into the work force, sometimes even before their children begin school. Thus, it is not remarkable to face the problem, as a middle-aged couple did in my office, of his depression about declining in his career at the same time she was enjoying the excitement of finishing her education and entering a new profession. It was quite difficult, because of their contrasting personal and professional situations, for them to be very sensitive and supportive of each other.

4. *Public and professional concern for physical and sexual abuse in marriage.* The well-kept secret about domestic abuse is a secret no longer. Physical and sexual abuse within marriage has become a matter of intense professional concern. Fortunately, a woman is much more likely now to receive the attention of a sympathetic professional if she goes to a police officer or a counselor to seek help because she is being beaten by her husband. Basic attitudes are changing among professional helpers, including clergy. Not long ago, if a woman went to a clergyman to say that her husband was assaulting her and she was afraid for her safety, the pastor would send her home with the admonition to "pray for your husband and be more submissive so you can make his life easier, because obviously he is under a lot of pressure to provide a living and a home for his family." Now the responsible professional helping person, clergy included, will consider referring the woman to a shelter, if necessary, and sending both partners to a center or agency that specializes in the treatment of domestic abuse. The emergence of greater public awareness in this critical area cannot but have a major impact on future marriages and help ensure safer marriages for more people.

5. *The rise in "blended families."* The consistently high incidence of divorce since World War II means that a greater number of single parents with children will remarry. Although the famous television family, the Brady Bunch, was portrayed as having a happy living arrangement, that is not typically the case for many blended families. Marriage with built-in children, often children in their teens, carries many hidden pitfalls. For example, the joining of two families can easily confuse parenting roles. The creation of a blended family is more than the union of two adults; it is frequently the merging of two quite different family histories and cultures. Nonetheless, if the blended family can be made to work, it offers a rich opportunity for some children, who might not otherwise have a family, to enjoy the advantages and the challenges of being reared in the security of a two-adult home.

6. *Increasing mobility and depersonalization within suburban culture.* Three decades ago Gibson Winter asserted, "We are the uprooted. We are the producers of things and the servants of machines. We live with things, ideas, and prices. We rarely have time to live with people."[3] The sprawling suburban culture of middle-class middle-management America shockingly reflects Winter's analysis. Living at a hectic pace just to stay even with their upwardly mobile neighbors, middle-class Americans are too busy to understand, much less to practice and experience, very much of the meaning of intimacy. Too often couples and their children only nod to each other as they pass outside the bathroom or in front of the refrigerator. Many families sit down together to a meal only three times a year: Christmas, Easter, and Thanksgiving. And for two of those meals, a televised football game may be turned on at the same time.

Within such a rootless and impersonal society, marriage loses some of its basic and essential anchors. The paradox is often true that married persons who cannot be intimate with others also cannot find intimacy between themselves. The loss of intimacy, and the inability to know how to find intimacy or create it, is the single greatest crisis facing modern marriage today.

The Pastor's Opportunity

Confronted by so many contemporary threats to the stability of modern marriages, what can a pastor do that will make any difference? It is commonplace for clergy to feel virtually powerless. Especially do they often despair at making a serious attempt at premarital counseling. Too many times a pastor may feel that a potential marriage is questionable but will go ahead with the ceremony because the couple would just go somewhere else to be married if this pastor did not do it. Likewise, when couples show signs of significant marital stress and strain, many clergy discount the significance of their role as intervenors in comparison with such other professionals as psychologists, psychiatrists, and social workers.

However, unlike other helping professionals, the pastor moves into people's lives with the authority of one who teaches the fundamental values that undergird marriage. Whether or not parishioners agree, they respect their pastor as someone who has knowledge, expertise, and authority in matters of values and faith. This authority is inherent in the pastoral office, even though we live in an age that is suspicious and questioning of most authority. Thus, it must be emphasized that intrinsic spiritual authority, coupled with the right of professional initiative, offers the pastor greater accessibility to troubled marriages than any other helping professional can claim. Speaking as a psychologist with many years' experience as a consultant to clergy, Paul Pruyser identified what he calls "the pastoral right of initiative and access" and asserted, "I have begged ministers always to be aware of this right as one of their most unique and valuable functional assets."[4]

Thomas Oden is equally convinced that the pastor's freedom and responsibility to be faithful in pastoral care and calling offers the pastor opportunities for early interventions that other professionals will never have.

> No office-bound psychiatrist is free to do this. This is why, at the level of accessibility, good pastoral counsel is potentially far more effective than secular, time-cramped, fee-based, medically modeled psychotherapies. Its accessibility offers it the opportunity to serve prior to the crisis. A timely intervention may prevent unnecessary hurt while promoting needed growth.[5]

Pastoral availability for marriage counseling occurs through more than just an active schedule of pastoral calling. Pastoral calling will undergird a ministry that addresses marital and relationship issues from a wide variety of pastoral opportunities. The pastors to whom parishioners will turn for marital help often engage in pastoral activities similar to the following:

Demonstrating in sermons and prayers both concern and sensitive understanding for the stresses encountered in marriage.

Offering brief study courses during the Sunday morning adult forum to aid the growth of marriages.

Leading a contract marriage growth group, which meets once a week to discuss a chapter from such books as *The Intimate Marriage* by Charlotte and Howard Clinebell.

If married, reflecting a marriage that is growing, vibrant, and joyful.

Being sufficiently open and self-revealing as to be seen by others as human and likely to be caring and nonjudgmental toward troubled marriages.

Finally, it must be said that the key ingredient for pastoral care in any context is pastoral initiative that is well informed by pastoral intuition. Such intuition is a matter of knowing when to go to a couple and say you are concerned for them and want to have a pastoral conversation with them. No other professional person has that right.

Sensitive pastoral initiative is not intrusive and does not violate any parishioner's privacy. When the need and the opportunity are obvious, pastoral initiative requires one to say, "I am your pastor and I care very much about you. Your marriage has too much pain and conflict. I would like to meet with both of you just as soon as it can be arranged." Because of their position, authority, and accessibility, clergy have a greater opportunity than any other group of professionals to bring a more promising outlook to the future of marriage in the coming decade.[6]

The Qualities of the Pastoral Marriage Counselor

The seasoned marital therapist has had much advanced training and supervision and in many cases has had personal psychotherapy to deepen self-understanding. By contrast, most parish pastors do not have anywhere near the level of specialized training of the clinical marriage therapist. But most parish clergy have the appropriate motivation, pastoral authority, and essential personality characteristics to offer care and help to the couples seeking their assistance. Although counseling specialists can easily point to the limitations of the average parish pastor as a counselor, the fact remains that, once ordained, a pastor is by definition a pastoral counselor, representing the church with all the rights and responsibilities that accompany ordination. Despite the very limited degree of training for all clergy in formal clinical skills and the obvious differences in counseling skills from pastor to pastor, it can hardly be questioned that the centuries-old Judeo-Christian tradition of the pastoral care of souls has offered as much benefit to humankind as any of the other helping disciplines, if not more.

Wayne Oates has identified three qualities that are basic to a helping relationship: an accurate empathy, a nonpossessive warmth, and an inherent genuineness.[7] Regardless of the level of the pastor's training, the aim will always be to exhibit those qualities identified by Oates.

The sign of *accurate empathy* is not for the counselor to say, "I understand what you are saying." No, the only authentic sign is when the counselee says, "Yes, you have understood me." The capacity to hear, comprehend, envision, and describe to the counselee the coun-selee's private world of perceptions and feelings is hard work. And most pastors should have the capacity to offer at least the basic, essential understanding necessary for their parishioners to be helped.

A *nonpossessive warmth* is genuine caring without strings attached. It has some of the qualities of that grace which always conveys caring and acceptance. Within the presence of such caring, a person who is conflicted will feel safe enough to reveal feelings that are hurtful. Non-possessive warmth invites us to be vulnerable so healing can take place. The message conveyed by such caring is that people are free to make their own choices without coercion or manipulation. Such grace is essential if pastoral counseling is to facilitate the resolution of marital conflict.

Genuineness in a pastoral counselor means that the pastor is honest with others and, just as important, honest with his or her own self and feelings. Such a counselor has integrity that is obvious and unquestion-able. In the presence of such a counselor, one knows that one will hear the truth. And when it is appropriate, the counselor will also be self-revealing without pretense or awkwardness. Genuineness is the capac-ity to face the truth within oneself as well as within others. Wayne Oates is correct; without genuineness, pastoral counselors will sound hollow and be ineffective despite how technically correct their interview techniques may be.

The effective pastoral counselor will also have many of the following personal qualities:

A genuine liking for people. Such a counselor is more interested in helping people than in slavishly following a certain counseling theory or technique.

An essentially positive feeling of self-worth. Such a counselor will be less likely to measure personal self-worth by personal "success" as a marriage counselor.

The ability to communicate without eliciting defensive reactions from others.

The ability to set boundaries in a professional manner, particularly for such things as length of counseling sessions and telephone con-versations.

The ability to live with ambiguity and unresolved conflict in others' marriages, knowing that despite the counselor's best efforts, not all couples will be helped.

Sufficient self-esteem and courage to be both honest and appro-priately assertive as a counselor.

A personal social support network, so counseling relationships are not used inappropriately for the pastor's social relationships.

A sense of prayer upon entering the counseling relationship.

The willingness to use outside persons or resources for consultation about counseling cases and situations.

An awareness of his or her own feelings and the ability to value them without discounting them.

The readiness to be a counselor to both spouses without taking sides.

The Pastor's Theology of Marriage

The pastor's theology is the primary value framework that shapes the pastor's counseling approach to troubled marriages. Pastors who do marriage counseling should reflect on those biblical passages that are informative about the nature of marriage. Those passages include:

Genesis 2:18–25
Exodus 20:1–17 (Deuteronomy 5:6–21)
Matthew 19:1–12 (Mark 10:1–12)
1 Corinthians 7:1–7 (8–40)
Ephesians 5:21–33
Colossians 3:18–19
Hebrews 13:4
1 Peter 3:1–7

Not included in this list is the prophet Hosea's marriage to Gomer as an object lesson for demonstrating the forgiving love of God for Israel. Likewise, Paul writing in Ephesians uses marriage as a unique relationship that helps to illustrate, by its essential mystery, the relationship of Christ to the church. Just as Jesus blessed the marriage at Cana in Galilee with his presence and the performance of his first miracle (John 2:1–11), so it is evident throughout scripture that marriage is held in the highest regard as the singularly unique relationship God has intended for a man and a woman to enjoy as partners for life.

The scriptural witness is clear that marriage, and with it the act of sexual intercourse, joins a man and a woman in a union different from any relationship they will have with any other person. For in becoming "one," they are not just affected emotionally or physically. Rather, it is an ontological new creation that includes their full being: wills, minds, feelings, values. And that fact of irrevocable connectedness with the other continues for the rest of their natural lives.

The radical nature of this new creation, and the total involvement of both persons with each other, cannot be overemphasized. Otto Piper states clearly the biblical view that the two marriage partners are indelibly changed through their permanent union.

Lying at the very center of the Biblical interpretation of sex we find the brief but significant sentence, "The two shall be one flesh" (Gen. 2:24). Three ideas in particular are expressed thereby:

1. Sexual intercourse establishes an inner union between the two persons concerned.

2. That union is a "unity of the flesh," i.e., it affects the vital wills of these persons.

3. This union can never be dissolved. . . .

The marriage vows cannot be construed as being valid only for the time that the relationship between the spouses is a "real" marriage. They are meant to keep the partners together through good and bad days alike. The ontological basis of marriage—the unity of the flesh—persists in spite of marital infidelity and even when there is no longer any love for the partner.[8]

Love in marriage is essentially living in harmony with oneself and with the partner who is one with you. The radical union that occurs through the marriage of two persons can be either a broken relationship or a relationship that reflects harmony and wholeness. Such wholeness does not exclude conflict; indeed, conflict in a loving relationship can lead to deeper wholeness.

Marital love, therefore, transcends passion, feeling, and romance. Of course, such love does not exclude the passionate dimension of marriage but in fact undergirds marital passion. The love described by Paul in 1 Corinthians 13:4–7 is certainly not rooted in the spontaneous and unpredictable impulses of emotion:

Love is patient and kind; love is not jealous or boastful; it is not arrogant or rude. Love does not insist on its own way; it is not irritable or resentful; it does not rejoice at wrong, but rejoices in the right. Love bears all things, believes all things, hopes all things, endures all things.

Such love between spouses is not ordinarily a matter of willpower. Indeed, human willpower generally falls far short when it comes to loving the unlovable. But the attitude, the frame of mind, to be loving toward one's spouse is essential to the nature of the marital union. Such loving commitment to the welfare of one's partner is acknowledged by most persons to be possible somehow by God's help and not as a result of their own virtue. For often in a marriage there are times when conflict overwhelms any human inclinations toward tenderness and kindness. And in those cases where the marital union continues over the years to thrive and endure, both persons have learned the maturity of loving the other in spite of each other's countless faults and limitations. Marriage that is lasting usually will reflect the love that cares for the other at least as much as one cares for oneself. Paul was right that such a love reflects a profound mystery, but Paul was also certain that that was how it should be: "Even so husbands should love their wives as their own bodies. He who loves his wife loves himself. For no man ever hates his own flesh" (Eph. 5:28–29a).

Those who have been well loved in their early, developing years, and who also are certain that they are loved by God, often have the greatest capacity to be loving to others. In marriage, love is essentially the joyous celebrating of "us," joined in a mysterious union they can never understand but which enlarges their lives far beyond their own single selves. The Clinebells have called such capacity for love "intimacy."

> We wish you the joy of ever more frequent moments when soul touches soul. Reaching toward each other, reaching up and reaching out together— always reaching, often touching, sometimes joining as "the new person— us," this is the intimacy of marriage.[9]

How, then, does the pastor take account of divorce from a theological point of reference? Jesus helps us when he answered a similar question put to him about divorce. Explaining Moses' permission of divorce, Jesus offered this explanation: "For your hardness of heart he wrote you this commandment" (Mark 10:5). In other words, scripture acknowledges the broken character of human motives, intentions, and relationships. And persons who are caught in the web of such brokenness, so the record tells us on good authority, are never beyond God's grace and God's intention for new hope, new beginning, and new creation.

If love is the transcending power that makes the ontological union of marriage functional, viable, workable, what other elements are primarily characteristic of the relationship? Because the marital union is a unique entity of its own, having its own being, certainly it participates in the essential qualities of all being. In that case, Paul Tillich's analysis of the ontological elements that constitute the basic structure of being is especially illuminating for the pastoral marriage counselor.

Tillich explains that those elements are essentially polar, holding together in a creative tension opposites that are necessary to each other. Those three polarities are individualization and participation, dynamics and form, and freedom and destiny.[10] Tillich asserts that it is not just life that has so many seemingly contradictory opposites but, in fact, it is being itself that has basic polar characteristics. Those opposites are always defining and redefining each other. And for that reason it is commonplace for the pastoral marriage counselor to be confronted with a multitude of competing themes in every marital relationship.

Individualization and participation. Sue and Phil had been married about three weeks when Sue had a telephone call from her close friend, Alice, who had also been married in the past month. Excited about her many wedding gifts, Alice asked Sue if she and Phil could come over to her house that night. Sue thought it was a fine idea. "Phil and I will be delighted to come over. We'll see you and Jim about seven thirty."

When Phil came home, Sue greeted him with her plans for the evening. "I told Alice we'd love to see their wedding gifts and that we'd be over at seven thirty. Won't that be fun?"

To Sue's dismay and, for that matter, to Phil's surprise as well, his response was a forthright "No!" The ensuing argument and subsequent conversation was revealing for both Sue and Phil. He did not want her making commitments for him or assuming she knew what his feelings, interests, or intentions might be, either for social engagements or for any other questions and issues. It was especially surprising for them to experience their deep feelings around this first crisis in their marriage, because they had assumed in their courtship that they were quite a bit alike. Sue thought she had good grounds for concluding that, if she wanted to see Alice and Jim's gifts, Phil would want to also. But Sue and Phil discovered very early a fact they would continue to encounter in their marriage: namely, that the two individuals God joins together will remain individuals—with some quite different feelings and ideas—throughout their marriage.

The joy of intimacy in marriage, which is participation at the deepest levels of human experience, cannot occur unless both partners have a firm sense of their own selfhood. If the boundaries for selfhood are not clear and secure, one spouse will be confronted with the anxiety of seeming to be overwhelmed by the other. Some persons will say to their spouse, "When I get too close to you, I lose who I am. I feel that you think for me and tell me what I should feel. I cease to exist in the shadow of your dominance." This is not satisfying and nurturing intimacy, because individualization has been sacrificed for accommodation and conformity, often under the excuse of avoiding conflict.

Individuality without participation also jeopardizes the integrity of marital intimacy. When Scott and Deborah came to their pastor, they complained that their mutual families often intruded into their marriage. As the pastor learned more about Scott and Deborah, it came to light that they were separated each year for two months at a time, when Scott would volunteer for a traveling assignment out of the country for his company. Neither person, and especially Scott, minded being separated for that long. Scott enjoyed the privacy, finding it a welcome relief not to be interrupted in his personal activities by Deborah's demands for attention. At other times Scott and Deborah would take separate vacations for a week or two in order to visit their own families. It soon became apparent to their pastor that Scott and Deborah did not have any depth to the bonds of intimacy in their marriage, and that their relationships with parents and siblings meant far more to them than their marital relationship. Their families were, indeed, intruding into the marriage mainly because Scott and Deborah had not formed a bond of intimacy between themselves built on participation as well as individualization. Scott and Deborah had married each other but had not really joined with each other; they did not have a truly intimate relationship. They were in fact living as roommates who happened also to be married.

Each couple will develop its own patterns for affirming individuality and joining together. It is a common practice for many couples to arrange, for example, that on Tuesday evenings she bowls with her girlfriends and on Thursday evenings he plays cards with the boys. One couple was surprised to discover that immediately after the joyous closeness of sexual intercourse, they occasionally had a little argument as they were lying in each other's arms. The deep intermingling of mind and spirit in the sexual union can quickly give way to a sudden awareness that "I am I and you are you, and I don't want you attacking or intruding on my turf!" Though such strong feelings may be surprising at such a moment, they in fact reflect a genuinely intimate relationship between two separate and distinct persons.

Writing in the Foreword to the Clinebells' book, counselor and educator Emily Hartshorne Mudd affirms the tension between individualization and participation that always characterizes marital intimacy. She asserts that "each partner in a marriage is unique and can be sufficiently secure to realize that difference can be constructive, stimulating, and even fun." She then illustrates this point by recalling Kahlil Gibran's poetic reminder that spouses need to experience their distinctness from each other in order to be partners in loving intimacy:

> But let there be spaces in your togetherness,
> And let the winds of the heavens dance between you.[11]

The continuing challenge for the pastoral counselor is to support the precious individuality of each spouse while also celebrating the inseparable dimensions and bonds in their marital union. Beyond that challenge, however, is the opportunity for helping both husband and wife to discover deeper meanings of intimacy because they are learning to be less dismayed by all the ways they really are quite different from each other.

Dynamics and form. Over twelve years ago John and Ann were married. They had not discussed their "contractual" relationship. They had understood that for them marriage would be a commitment, but they had not talked about their particular roles as husband and wife and how they would relate with each other. Ann had known that John would be going to graduate school, and once or twice they talked together about their plans for Ann to be the primary income earner until John got his degree. This meant they would delay having children until John had finished his education.

John's father had died when he was in grade school, and later John and his mother went to live with her mother, John's grandmother. So John was, in effect, reared by two women who were quite attentive to his needs. Certainly John's laundry and ironing had always been done for him, and he never had to worry about cooking any meals. In Ann's family, her mother had taken the role of traditional housewife, cooking the meals, doing the laundry, and keeping the house clean. So there seemed to be no difficulty for John and Ann to begin their marriage with John busy as a graduate student and Ann holding a full-time job as well as doing the cooking, laundry, and cleaning for both of them. John helped in the kitchen, but the domestic chores continued to be mainly Ann's responsibility.

Eight years after John finished graduate school, Ann went to her pastor for help. She felt very upset—about her marriage and her relationship with her two children, ages seven and six. She told her pastor that she did not understand what was happening inside of her. Moreover, Ann felt very guilty about her anger. Her self-image was of a "traditional" woman who is a faithful housewife and homemaker. Yet she felt angry that she had to take care of two children and a husband, cleaning up after them seven days a week. "John does so little around the house," she exclaimed, "I often feel like I'm taking care of *three* children!" Ann's pastor immediately recognized that marriage counseling was necessary, if John could be persuaded to participate.

John and Ann's marriage had changed: slowly, imperceptibly, but unquestionably. And the change had created pain, which, at the moment, Ann was feeling more acutely than John. However, John came to feel pain and anxiety also as Ann made her attempts, with her pastor's help, to find relief for her emotional distress.

Tillich helps us understand that it is the nature and structure of being to remain constant while at the same time transcending itself as it becomes something new. Certainly this ontological polarity called dynamics and form is very evident in marriage. Tillich's words sound as if they were written particularly to describe the changes that occur in the marital relationship.

> Therefore, it is impossible to speak of being without also speaking of becoming. Becoming is just as genuine in the structure of being as is that which remains unchanged in the process of becoming. And, vice versa, becoming would be impossible if nothing were preserved in it as the measure of change.[12]

Hardly five minutes after a man and a woman have taken their marriage vows, their relationship has begun to change in the process of growth toward its full potential. And every five minutes thereafter their relationship will be changing because that is the nature of all being. Both partners will be changing as individuals, and so will the multitude of ways they interact with each other. Clifford Sager has described those changing, hidden dynamics as the conscious and unconscious contracts that all married partners have between themselves. Sager has gone so far as to identify at least forty-one different aspects of marriage within which fundamental change can occur, and in which couples will be helped if they can recognize their expectations of each other in those areas. He explains how such changes can result in serious conflict for a couple:

> Each partner feels that *in exchange for what he* [sic] *will give to the other he will receive what he wants*. However, each partner is operating on a different set of contractual terms, and each is unaware of the other's terms. Further, contractual terms change as the marriage goes on, different stages of the life cycle are attained, and outside forces impinge on the couple as a pair or on either individual. Hence, contractual terms or rules of the game are often changed by one spouse without discussion, and certainly without the consent of the other.[13]

Not all change results in pain, but much change in human life and relationships is very stressful. A basic question for the pastor doing marriage counseling is how that pastor will regard the dynamic changes evident in parishioners' marriages. In John and Ann's case, some pastors might tell Ann to return home and seek the Lord's help in continuing the traditional domestic pattern she has followed all the years of her marriage. However, such a response would fail to take account of the powerful and healthy forces for change occurring within both John and Ann and in their marriage. On the other hand, a counseling approach that affirms Tillich's insights would take account of the pain in marital growth as well as the enormous potential for hope as a marriage relationship grows in exciting new directions.

Each marriage has its own "form"—its own relationship patterns, history, interaction of needs, desires, and personality characteristics. The keystone, the single essential element, is the continuing decision by each partner to remain committed to the marriage through all the changes that the years bring.

The contractual terms of every marriage will often be modified, and the challenge for the pastoral counselor is always to see if there is any honest basis for helping both partners to say to each other, "I still want to be married to you." All else can change, but that commitment must remain intact if a marriage is to last through periods of painful marital strife and growth.

Marriage relationships are extraordinarily dynamic, and for that reason every married couple can be dismayed on occasion by the changes occurring between them. At other times the same couple will rejoice with the increasing maturity and newfound depths of love they share as more years pass. If such dynamic change were not the rule, marriage could very soon become a terribly boring enterprise indeed!

Freedom and destiny. Betsy and David had had disturbing episodes of conflict for most of the seven years they were married. Several times one or the other had threatened to leave. Then one evening when David returned home from work remembering the painful arguments of the last three nights and expecting the usual tension to envelop him as he walked through the door, he sensed that something was terribly different. The house was very quiet. His children did not run to greet him, and Betsy was not in the kitchen fixing supper. Quick glances in every room confirmed his worst fear. Betsy and the children were gone!

David survived for the five days his family was away, but they were the most dreadful five days of his life. Betsy phoned David once to tell him she was safe, but she would not reveal where she and the children were staying. David was greatly relieved the day he came home from work and saw Betsy's car in the driveway. He sighed a prayer of thanksgiving that his family had returned home safely.

In the weeks following Betsy's return, David hardly let her out of his sight. Whenever she left the house, he insisted on knowing where she was going, how long she would be there, whom she would be with, and when she would be returning. His anxiety about losing her was threatening to get out of hand. Ironically, his excessively possessive behavior, prompted by his fears of losing Betsy, were coming close to driving her away from him permanently. She was fast coming to feel imprisoned and smothered, and was finding herself thinking more and more about divorce as the only way to gain freedom and sanity.

Many pastors have encountered similar situations. When couples like Betsy and David come into a pastor's office, one spouse will invariably protest that the right to freedom has been lost, and the other spouse will assert with equal vehemence that, because one is married, one no longer has any right to exercise such freedom as leaving the home.

Tillich, in describing the third ontological polarity as that of freedom and destiny, asserts that "Man [sic] is man because he has freedom, but he has freedom only in polar interdependence with destiny." Then Tillich discusses how freedom is experienced as deliberation, followed by decision, with responsibility or accountability for one's decisions. One's destiny, on the other hand, includes all of one's former decisions (such as vows of faithfulness and commitment) as well as what is going to happen in the future.[14] Marriage, as an ontological entity of its own, expresses the polarity of freedom and destiny because it participates in and reflects the freedom and destiny of both parties to the marriage.

When two persons marry, they do not give up their freedom. Their choice-making remains intact, despite the tradition of so-called bachelor parties which celebrate the groom's supposed last taste of freedom for the rest of his life. Once married, both spouses have simply and voluntarily changed the context within which they will continue to exercise their freedom. They are still just as free within marriage to deliberate, decide, and be responsible for their decisions. The fact that ontologically each spouse is free does not negate or diminish the earlier decisions and vows to be husband and wife. Those vows are part of their destiny, upon which further decisions will be made.

The freedom Betsy and David have to remain in their marriage or to leave is not a matter of having a "right" to leave or stay. Freedom for making choices is inherent to marriage and to each individual person, not as a right but as an essential characteristic of being human and being married.

In many marriages the issue of freedom does not express itself as a consideration of divorce but rather as a matter of control. Most spouses try somehow to control and manipulate their partner. It is basic to human nature to try to manage a relationship in order to ensure that one's own needs will always be met. Perhaps this human tendency is particularly evident when two people marry with the intention of changing each other's annoying habits once the ceremony is over.

Most efforts to change another person in any manner will end in frustration and failure. Human beings change when they have the opportunity to respond in freedom. And of course, within the context of such freedom, there can be no guarantee about exactly *how* they will change. Freedom obviously cannot be used as a guise for control. But two partners cannot affirm each other's inherent, ontological freedom unless they affirm, at the same time, their own anxiety about their partner's freedom. The most honest statement either married partner can make is, "I cannot control your choice to stay married to me, and I cannot control the person you are or the person you will become. Yet, despite not having those guarantees, I still choose to be your marriage partner." Hardly any other affirmation can take more courage: the courage, indeed, required for being married.

The pastor who can affirm each partner's inherent freedom will be supporting what most people already sense to be true about themselves and about their marriage. Thus, by recognizing and supporting each spouse's freedom for decision and responsibility, the pastor will help to create a situation in which both persons are more likely to want to find a way to remain happily and satisfactorily married.

The Theological Context of Pastoral Marriage Counseling

On what theological grounds does the pastor have the courage and the confidence to sit down in the presence of a troubled, conflicted couple? How does a pastor justify attempting to be a healing resource for relationships where there has been painful misunderstanding for most of the marriage? For most clergy, any such justification cannot be based on their specialized training, because they have hardly had any specialized training. The legitimate basis for pastoral marriage counseling rests in the unique theological and faith context within which that counseling event occurs.

In 1961 Seward Hiltner and Lowell G. Colston published their study *The Context of Pastoral Counseling,* in which they reported their research into whether people who seek help from a pastor in a pastoral setting may make more, or more rapid, progress than if they seek another type of counselor. Hiltner and Colston asserted that the context of pastoral counseling was the distinguishing factor between the counseling done by ministers and the counseling done by other professional persons. Context was then further defined as having four dimensions: the setting within a church, the expectations counselees have of a minister, the shift from a general pastoral relationship to a special helping relationship, and the pastor's self-imposed limitations regarding time, skill, and training.[15]

However, of equal or greater importance than those factors reported by Hiltner and Colston is the theological context within which the minister functions as a marriage counselor. That faith context is the Word, which is the ground of all words that bring healing and reconciliation. From John's Gospel we have learned that for God the communication of being, of God's being of saving power and love, is through the *logos,* the Word (John 1:1–5). Jesus Christ, we believe, is that singularly unique Word of communication of God's being. Jesus is the Word of reconciliation. And where words of communication from the being of one person to the being of another person result in reconciliation, it is not the pastor's accomplishment but rather the work of that Word which is always reconciling, recreating new life and new hope for relationships.[16]

Biblically, words are empowered to be instruments for saving and reconciling encounters. They are never just words. The words of encounter bring together being with being. And always in such meetings there is the potential for persons to be greatly changed. Moses encountered a burning bush and heard the words, "Do not come near; put off your shoes from your feet, for the place on which you are standing is holy ground" (Ex. 3:5). After that encounter Moses was never the same.

Nor was Jacob after his wrestling encounter and exchange of words at the turning point of his life (Gen. 32:22–32), nor David after hearing the words of Nathan's accusation (2 Sam. 12:1–23), nor Saul of Tarsus on his way to Damascus, hearing the words he would never forget, "I am Jesus, whom you are persecuting" (Acts 9:1–9).

Not all words result in healing and reconciliation. Unfortunately, many couples know firsthand that words can be destructive and hurtful. That is why troubled couples find their way to the pastor's office. Often these couples say, "We have a communication problem." Words cannot bring healing (a) when they are not heard and (b) when the words do not communicate from being to being. But the pastoral marriage counselor believes that all words spoken in the context of the Word, the being of God's presence, have the potential for resulting in reconciliation.

Though obvious, it must be said that the context of God's Word is not confined to the four walls of the pastor's office or to the building called a church. Nor is God's reconciling work confined to pastors; God's Word of reconciliation is also present with so-called secular marriage counselors.

Words that communicate the being of one person to another are always words of truth. Such words tell the truth about one's motives, intentions, hopes, and feelings. Words do not often communicate very well when they are used in an attempt to describe or analyze the other person. Words that best communicate truth will ordinarily be limited to describing one's own person and being. Those words about oneself will not always be positive words; sometimes they will convey uncertainty, ambiguity, despair, and pessimism. When a pastor enables such words of truth to be spoken, the pastor is performing a function particularly characteristic of pastoral counseling and is doing the most any counselor can do.

The pastor's other task is to make it possible for words of truth to be heard. In pastoral marriage counseling, such words are to be spoken in a context of respect in which persons are valued and not attacked, respected and not belittled. When words conveying truth are spoken within such a context of respectful love, the potential is always greater that those words of truth will be heard for reconciliation and healing.

Pastoral marriage counseling is always a basically hopeful undertaking. This statement could not be made if it were not for the faith context within which the counseling takes place. Such hope takes account of all the realities and never glosses over the most negative aspects of a conflicted marriage. But when two persons who have not been talking to each other so they can be heard finally sit down together in the presence of a pastor, there is always the dynamic potential that they themselves and their relationship will be changed for the better. Such hopeful change is especially possible when the counseling takes account of the most negative aspects of the marriage.

Fred had been in his own place for three weeks before Sharon finally persuaded him to come with her to see their pastor, Clayton Thompson. Talking with both of them together, and later in an individual session with Fred, Thompson saw clearly that Fred held virtually no hope of any reconciliation with his wife. He felt badly that he and Sharon were breaking up their marriage and their family, but the pain of years of conflict and misunderstanding had taken too great a toll of Fred's emotions. Now, living alone in a small, barely furnished room, he found a sense of peace that was a great relief to him from the tension he always felt in his stomach whenever he and Sharon tried to talk to each other. At first glance, there was little or no basis for hope in such a troubled marriage. Usually, under such circumstances, one can expect one or both spouses to use the counseling simply to confirm the conclusion they have already reached that divorce is unavoidable.

Because the faith context of pastoral marriage counseling always offers a basis for hope, Pastor Thompson's strategy was to find a truthful and honest means for Fred and Sharon, through counseling, to continue their dialogue. So Thompson affirmed Fred's deeply held reservations and suggested that Fred and Sharon return, not for marriage counseling but simply for "communication counseling."

Renaming the counseling did not fundamentally change what their pastor wanted to accomplish. But suggesting to Fred that he and Sharon come together essentially to learn how to talk to each other, while Fred continued to live outside the home, helped both Fred and Sharon to be honest about how deeply troubled their marriage really was. Now they could meet with their pastor without feeling that either had given in or that their serious problems had been discounted. But they would be meeting in the context of hope, even though all three of them considered it premature to call their conversations marriage counseling.

Pastor Thompson could have taken either of two other approaches. He could have decided that if Fred and Sharon did not want "marriage counseling," there were no grounds for hope that anything positive might be accomplished. Thompson might then have offered to counsel separately with both Fred and Sharon as they worked out their separation and divorce. Or Thompson might have offered a groundless hope, telling Fred that things were not so bad and that if he moved back home the marital problems would soon be resolved. But neither of these two approaches would have taken account of the need for affirming the truth about the extensive problems in the marriage, or recognized the realistic basis for hope that is present when honest dialogue does take place. Thompson's strategy of renaming the counseling offered an honest basis for Fred and Sharon to begin the difficult process of a dialogue that held some promise, in the distant future, for reconciliation.

Now, having a hope based on the faith context of pastoral marriage counseling, the next step for the pastor is "How?" The following chapters specifically address that question. The focus of the discussion centers on a structured approach for a short-term pastoral intervention in troubled marriages. The aim is to offer pastors a model for marriage counseling that reflects a biblical and theological understanding of marriage while also taking account of the unique and limited resources that parish pastors have to offer as marriage counselors.

2
INITIATING SHORT-TERM MARRIAGE COUNSELING

The overall goal of marriage crisis counseling and also marriage therapy is to help couples learn how to make their relationship more mutually need-satisfying and therefore more growth-nurturing.

—Howard Clinebell[1]

When a pastor hears words that convey the urgent message, "Our marriage is in trouble," the immediate question is how to respond appropriately to what often is a very painfully conflicted relationship. To this human crisis the pastor brings the authority of the pastoral office, the rich heritage of the Judeo-Christian tradition of the care of souls, and a heart filled with loving concern undergirded with the wisdom of experience and observation. Also, a pastor may bring some formal training from such settings as clinical pastoral education. All of that is more than enough to enable the pastor to intervene in the midst of human conflict, offering hope and proposing a practical strategy for seeking resolution.

A Model for Brief Pastoral Marriage Counseling

The goal of the model for short-term pastoral marriage counseling is to offer a pattern that most pastors can follow for intervening effectively in troubled marriages. The aim is not to guarantee that a pastor's counselees will always go away with happy and conflict-free marriages. Instead, the purpose of this model is to make it possible for pastors to offer a hopeful plan for working on marital problems, to be present with a couple when difficult decisions must be made, and to have enough information for helping a couple to consider possible longer-term counseling with the pastor or with another professional resource.

In many instances, short-term intervention can be very helpful to enable a couple to interrupt destructive patterns in their marriage.

David Mace has long been widely recognized as a caring and effective marriage counselor. After many years of this work, Mace suffered a severe heart attack. Following his recovery from that serious threat to his life, Mace was forced to reduce his professional involvement. Because of those necessary constraints, Mace adopted a new pattern for his counseling. Instead of seeing couples for months and months, he saw them for briefer periods, sometimes as limited as a single two-hour session. Referring to himself in the third person, Mace records his surprising discovery:

> Looking back over some 35 years of professional marriage counseling, he is aware that he has wasted a great deal of time (his own and that of his clients) working doggedly on situations which offered little room for improvement, and by allowing clients to go on talking while they avoided action. He believes that the counseling he has done under the severe limitations imposed on him during the past three years has, because of his adoption of more streamlined approaches, actually been more effective than previous efforts.[2]

Mace is not alone among experienced therapists in deciding that brief counseling can be an effective model for helping marriages. In describing his own rationale for short-term therapy with families, Joel Bergman has outlined an approach that can be adopted by pastors for their counseling interventions. Bergman uses the language of a roadside repair service in order to make his point.

> My posture toward psychotherapy and toward myself as a therapist is to see what I do as emergency road service. I assume that people and families come into treatment because they are stuck somewhere on their own roads. They have tried to solve their problems by themselves and have not been able to do so. They are also somewhat demoralized because their attempted solutions have failed. My job is to get these people back on the road as quickly as possible. As I tell my patients, I do not do tuneups, overhauls, or bodywork—I just do whatever is needed to get that car back on the road. If people want more after that, I will refer them to specialists who do tuneups, overhauls, or bodywork. Occasionally, I do overhauls myself, based upon a request and my agreement at the outset of therapy, but my basic posture as a therapist is to get people out of therapy as quickly as possible.[3]

With many couples, short-term intervention can be the most effective and appropriate form of pastoral counseling. Such brief marriage counseling should be well within the range of capability for most pastors, and often many troubled couples will not choose to remain in counseling for more extensive therapy. Moreover, most clergy recognize they cannot justify devoting more of their pastoral time to doing longer-term counseling.

Brief pastoral marriage counseling can be done following a structured five-stage model that involves five to seven sessions with the couple, both individually and together. The sessions typically last from fifty to sixty minutes and are generally scheduled once a week.

The Model

1. *The invitation to couple counseling.* Through contact initiated by themselves or their pastor, one or both spouses make it known that their marriage is in trouble. The pastor invites the couple to come together to the first marriage counseling session.

2. *The initial session with the couple.* Both spouses are seen together so they can discuss with their pastor in each other's presence the problems that are causing conflict in their relationship. In preparation for subsequent sessions, the pastor gives each spouse a questionnaire that will supply essential background information about each partner and their relationship. (The Pastoral Marriage Counseling Questionnaire follows chapter 5.)

3. *Individual sessions with each spouse.* The pastor sees each spouse separately for one or two counseling sessions.

4. *Both spouses seen together.* In a single session, the pastor helps the couple assess the learnings or insights gained thus far in the counseling process.

5. *The final session.* The purpose of this session is for the pastor and the couple to evaluate the progress made toward resolving the marital conflicts. At this meeting the pastor will recommend one of three options: termination of counseling, referral to another counselor, or recontracting with the pastor for further counseling sessions.

Any model has its strengths and its limitations. If a pastoral counseling model is to be effective, it should be based on sound theory and theological reflection, and it should also be practical for wide use in parish counseling situations. Exceptions can always be found that will not fit the full application of a model, and in those instances only selected elements of the model may be used. This outline for brief pastoral marriage counseling is not intended to be followed slavishly but, rather, is offered as an approach to be used prudently. The assumption behind the model is that it offers an effective and sound approach for most parish pastors to intervene in the marriage crises of many of their parishioners.

The strengths of the model. The structured five-stage pastoral marriage counseling model offers several benefits to a parish pastor, regardless of the experience a pastor may or may not have. Eight benefits are listed here.

1. *A hopeful and realistic plan for a troubled couple.* A severely conflicted marriage is a very upsetting crisis for both spouses. When persons are in crisis, the best pastoral intervention is to offer an immediate solution, if possible, or to outline a strategy so the couple has clear, realistic steps to follow toward the promise of a resolution. It is possible that a couple may come to a pastor and, in one session, find a solution to their marital crisis. However, in most instances a pastor will offer the best help by outlining the brief marriage counseling model and assuring the couple that the short-term process will help both of them make their own best decisions about what can be done to help their marriage. Thus the couple is invited to undertake a definite course of action that holds the promise of gaining better understanding of their crisis, finding resolution, or continuing with the pastor or another professional in longer-term marriage counseling. Although a couple usually will not leave after the first counseling session with any solutions to their problems, they can depart with a hopeful strategy that involves both of them working together over a specific number of weeks for the improvement of their marriage.

2. *A source of confidence for the pastor.* It should not be surprising that a pastor's first reaction to hearing a couple's marital problems would be, "Oh no, what do I do now?" The second common reaction for many pastors is to feel that an immediate solution must be found before the three of them can leave the counseling session. This sense of desperation has led many pastors to sit for several hours in a couple's kitchen, drinking coffee until 12:30 or 1:00 A.M., in search of a solution that eludes them. In most instances a solution cannot be found right away because the couple's problems may have been fifteen years in the making and involve many complex motivations, needs, and feelings in both partners.

However, in the face of such complexity a pastor now can offer to almost any couple the brief marriage counseling model as a road map, which holds out the possibility of leading them to an eventual resolution of their relationship difficulties. The pastor's confidence is not that a simple, quick solution will be found. Rather, his or her assurance is based on a strategy that can be helpful regardless of whatever level of counseling experience the pastor may have.

3. *A plan for both pastoral assessment and counseling.* The brief marriage counseling model will enable the pastor to collect necessary data as well as help some couples to make important changes in a short amount of time. The pastoral counselor is always engaged in making an assessment and then designing appropriate counseling interventions. The model offers the pastor several opportunities for gathering data on which to make at least tentative decisions for action and recommendation. The questionnaire that is distributed to the couple at the end of the first session elicits essential information that will help any counselor or therapist in making a careful assessment. Moreover, the short-term model not only provides necessary data for the pastor, it also will help many couples to achieve quite significant progress on their problems in a limited period of time.

For example, after spending part of an evening completing the questionnaire, a counselee may report to the pastor, "It took me quite a while to fill out that form you gave us, but it set me to thinking about things I had not thought about before. It was even helpful just to be able to put my thoughts and feelings on paper. Our problems look less complicated now."

4. *A structured counseling intervention.* The brief marriage counseling model assumes that structure in pastoral counseling is a major factor for the healing and reconciliation of broken relationships. Thus the structure of the model outlines the number and nature of the counseling sessions, the sequence in which certain steps are followed, the frequency of the sessions (usually one a week), and the length of the sessions (fifty to sixty minutes each). A pastor can make significant progress within those limits and most likely will accomplish whatever is possible within the space of one to two months. Such progress often occurs because couples may be more likely to focus their energy and their attention toward resolution of conflict when they know they have contracted for a certain limited number of counseling sessions. Furthermore, the discipline of a structured approach will help most pastors to avoid the pitfalls of aimless counseling that invests many tiring hours but heads in no definite direction. Such unstructured pastoral counseling can easily lead to the frustration and despair of the couple and the weariness and disappointment of the pastor. The structured pattern of the brief marriage counseling model offers the greatest likelihood for those unfortunate consequences to be avoided in the parish setting.

5. *An affirmation of the spouses' unity and individuality.* Effective marriage counseling takes account of two fundamental characteristics of a marriage: namely, that in a marriage the couple is united as one and, also, that a marriage is a union of two persons whose uniqueness as separate individuals is always an integral part of the relationship. In many of the sessions the focus is on the relationship itself as the pastor sees both spouses at the same time. However, it is equally essential that the pastor also have one or two individual sessions with each spouse, as the third step in the counseling process. Individual sessions make it all the more obvious to the pastor that each spouse usually sees the marriage problems from a unique perspective. Also, the individual counseling sessions help both husband and wife to reflect alone on the marriage without the defensiveness and emotionality that typically occur when they are in the presence of their partner. Particularly important is the opportunity in individual sessions for the pastor to ask each person what he or she is prepared or willing to change personally in order to improve the marriage. By including both joint and individual counseling sessions in the process, the brief marriage counseling model draws on the couple's fullest potential for finding resolution to their marital crisis.

6. A flexible vehicle for the pastor's theology and counseling style. A basic assumption for the brief pastoral marriage counseling model is that pastors have their own theology of marriage, and that they also have a wide variety of counseling experience and interviewing styles. Despite these differences among pastors, the structured brief marriage counseling model can be used effectively by most all clergy who are persuaded that the structured approach represents their best opportunity for helping couples. Also, the model does not assume that a pastor has had even a minimal degree of formal clinical training. Pastors without any further training in counseling beyond their seminary education will be able to help many couples through the use of the brief counseling model.

7. A beneficial approach regardless of available referral resources. Although many clergy serve in or near metropolitan areas where there are usually good professional resources to which couples can be referred, there are also many pastors who serve in outlying areas where referral resources are sometimes less reliable. In either case, the brief marriage counseling model offers important options.

When referral resources are either questionable or too far away to be used, the brief counseling model will enable pastors to offer effective counseling intervention and help that otherwise would not be available at all. Pastors can now begin to help couples make significant changes for the better in relationships that otherwise could continue for years with deep pain and emotional scarring for both partners.

In areas where reliable professional counseling resources are readily available, many troubled couples still do not use those resources until a person they trust, such as their pastor, makes the initial intervention and referral. In such cases, the brief marriage counseling model helps a couple recognize more clearly the actual depth and complexity of the marital crisis and provides an opportunity for the pastor, at the end of the process, to make a referral that the couple will trust and follow.

8. An effective intervention for most marital crises. There is hardly any marital crisis for which the brief marriage counseling model does not offer appropriate counseling intervention. In most instances, couples will be greatly helped by the structured process, which enables them to take time to consider carefully the deeper issues and complexities that contribute to their marital conflict.

However, there are notable situations in which some action must be taken immediately. In cases where there is the threat of physical abuse or severe emotional abuse, a counseling process that extends over four to eight weeks may only place one or both spouses in continued or greater danger. A wise pastor will help one or both spouses to make immediate decisions so such abuse cannot occur, or make an intervention and referral so the abusing spouse enters professional treatment for the abusive behavior. The advantage of the brief marriage counseling model is its flexibility, which permits a prompt referral to other professional counselors at any point in the process.

The limitations of the model. It is important to be fully aware of the basic limitations inherent in the brief pastoral marriage counseling model. Although the model offers a sound approach for pastors to help the greatest number of distressed couples, it will not be adequate or applicable in all circumstances. Three general areas of limitation should be noted.

1. *Not all couples will find resolution to their marital conflicts through this model.* First of all, it is quite evident to experienced counselors that not all conflicted couples will find help through *any* counseling approach. Some marriages will end in divorce despite the best efforts of professional counselors, and some persons seem intent upon resisting or defeating any outside professional help. Indeed, experienced pastors also know that spouses may come to marriage counseling with the single purpose of finding approval for the divorce they have already decided to obtain. So the brief marriage counseling model has the same limitation of any counseling model or approach: no way has yet been found to help *every* marriage that is in trouble.

Moreover, pastors will encounter couples or individuals who will be reluctant to cooperate with certain aspects of the short-term model presented in this book. For example, despite the pastor's best efforts, both spouses may refuse to come together to the first joint session. One spouse may be willing, but the other may refuse. Or, if they both do come to the initial session, one or both may decide not to continue with the future counseling sessions proposed by the pastor. The pastor may hear the ultimatum, "I'll come one more time with her, Pastor, but if you can't help us by then, this counseling is a waste of time!"

Also, it is conceivable that a couple's level of conflict may in fact be more intense after following the short-term model than it was when they first came to the pastor. They may report to the pastor that the five counseling sessions only opened old wounds, so their marital problems are worse now than they were before. Such cases do not necessarily reflect a limitation of the brief counseling model; rather, they indicate the deeper complexities of a marital conflict that could hardly fail to be uncovered through the short-term counseling approach. A pastor simply needs to realize that at the final counseling session the couple's evaluation may be that no progress has been made. Such an evaluation, while probably accurate, will often reflect far more the depth of the marital conflict than the adequacy of the counseling model or the pastor's counseling skills.

Many troubled couples will need further counseling beyond the sessions outlined in the brief marriage counseling model. It would be a misuse of the short-term model to use it for applying Band-Aids to severely conflicted marriages. A pastor should always be sensitive to the actual depth of the marital conflict, remembering that a referral to another resource is an appropriate option at the last session or at any time in the counseling process.

2. The level of the pastor's counseling skills is a limiting factor. The brief marriage counseling model assumes that every pastor who is willing to extend pastoral care to parishioners with conflicted marriages has at least adequate counseling skills to make good use of the short-term model. This assumption is based on the fact that once a pastor is ordained, that pastor is by virtue of the pastoral office a pastoral counselor and a "shepherd of souls" in the centuries-old tradition of the church.

But not all pastors are equally skilled as counselors. The brief marriage counseling model is limited by the skill of those who use it. No model, even if it has an unquestionably sound theoretical and theological basis, can make up for insensitive and thoughtless counseling. Pastors who bring a caring and prayerful attitude to their counseling will be able to make good use of the short-term model. But the model will prove quite inadequate when used by pastors who cannot communicate a basic warmth toward their parishioners and a sincere desire to help them reach their own better understanding of God's purpose and will for themselves and for their marriage.

3. The Pastoral Marriage Counseling Questionnaire will be too sophisticated for some persons. The questionnaire that the pastor gives to the couple at the end of the first joint session provides an efficient means for the pastor to gather data essential to the counseling process. But some counselees may be threatened or overwhelmed by the prospect of a form, several pages long, that asks them to write responses to questions asking for personal and intimate information about themselves.

The questionnaire may be especially difficult for persons with a limited formal education. Such persons may more easily be able to verbalize their answers to the pastor than to translate their thoughts into written words. In other cases, counselees may not be able to complete the questionnaire because certain questions evoke strong and disturbing feelings that cannot easily be put on paper. In such instances, the pastoral counselor will be wise to restrict the use of the questionnaire and, instead, ask questions during the individual counseling sessions to obtain data that otherwise would have been gathered through written responses.

The Invitation to Couple Counseling

The pastor's invitation begins the process through which a couple engages in marital counseling. That invitation can occur in a variety of circumstances and may take several different forms. In any event, the invitation is the pastor's way of expressing care and concern and demonstrates that the pastor is prepared to offer professional assistance.

In some instances the pastor's invitation is no more than a matter of putting an appointment in the calendar book. Rodney Smith called the church office Monday morning and was relieved to find that Pastor Jim Tate was available.

Rodney: Hello, Pastor Tate? I'm glad I reached you this morning. Last night Sally and I were talking about your sermon on family life. And—uh, we both agreed that it's time for us to talk with you about some problems we've been having in our own marriage. Could we see you sometime this week?

Pastor: I'm glad you called, Rodney. I'd be more than happy to see you and Sally. Let's see.... I have Tuesday or Wednesday evening open. I could see you both for about an hour on one of those evenings: say, at seven. Would either of those times be convenient?

Rodney: Wednesday at seven would be fine. I'm glad you can see us so soon. We were afraid your schedule would be filled up.

Pastor: Thank you for calling. I'll look forward to seeing you and Sally in my office Wednesday evening at seven.

In this pastoral exchange Tate expressed gratitude and openness to Rodney for making the phone contact. It was evident to Rodney that his pastor wanted to respond as soon as possible. However, it is important to note that Pastor Tate did not feel it necessary to engage in further counseling over the telephone or to ask probing questions about Rodney's views of the marital problems. The opportunity for those questions comes when Rodney and Sally are together in their pastor's office on Wednesday evening.

More often, the invitation to couple counseling occurs after the pastor has taken some specific initiative. For example, Pastor Harold Kline was making a call one evening in the home of Allan and Nancy Brown to talk with them about the baptism of their baby at next Sunday's worship service. While he was discussing the details and meaning of the baptism of their child, it was natural for Allan and Nancy to talk about other concerns, such as Nancy's anxieties about her mother's failing health and Allan's worries about possibly being laid off from his job. It was soon evident to their pastor that Allan and Nancy were under so much stress that it could also be affecting their marriage.

Pastor: I'm concerned about the pressures you're both feeling these days. Do you ever find that stress makes it hard for you to get along with each other without being impatient or edgy?

Nancy: Frankly, I *am* worried about that. Recently I've been feeling a new distance beginning to come between Allan and me.

Allan: Sometimes when I come home from work I just don't feel like talking, and it seems those are always the times Nancy gets after me with a lot of questions.

Pastor: Right now you're involved with your plans for the baptism next Sunday, and you have company coming from out of town for the weekend. But after everyone has gone home, I'm wondering if I could see you both in my office so we could talk some more about how things are going with your relationship in the midst of so many pressures. Would you both be willing to do that?

Allan: Nancy, if you're willing, I think I am. Maybe it would be a help to talk some more about how what is going on right now affects our marriage.

Nancy: These aren't easy things to talk about, but I'm willing. Sometimes I get worried about where we might be heading.

Because the marital crisis was not overwhelming, Pastor Kline stayed with the original purpose of the evening—preparation for the baptism—and did not immediately begin marriage counseling. But he was sensitive to the pressures and stresses affecting the Browns' marriage and gathered enough information from them to make the invitation for a marriage counseling session the next week.

Pastor Kline's invitation grew out of alert and empathetic pastoral listening. Occasions for making a similar invitation occur in many church-related settings. The pastor who listens carefully at council or deacon meetings, or in the course of routine pastoral calling, will often hear clues that a marriage is under extraordinary stress. At the right moment in a private conversation with one or both partners, a concerned pastor can invite the couple to come together to the pastor's office so the three of them can explore how the relationship might be helped or improved.

It is not unusual for people to come to their pastor alone with the express purpose of discussing their marriage and their disappointments about what they see as their partner's failures. Jeanne Phelps's conversation with Pastor Phyllis Wilson in her office will be familiar to most pastors.

Jeanne: Since Clark got this new job, he might as well never come home. He takes no responsibility around the house or with the kids. In fact, when he *is* home I feel like I've just got one more kid to take care of, and I sure don't need that!

Pastor: Jeanne, you're tired of things the way they are between you and Clark, and you feel something has to change. However, you and I cannot change Clark or how you relate to one another if Clark is not here too. I would really like to see you both together. As soon as possible, let's arrange a time that will be convenient for all of us.

Jeanne: I suppose you're right, but I don't know if Clark will come. He doesn't do anything anymore that I want him to do.

Pastor: Will you ask him? Please tell him that you spoke to me today and I said it is important for him to come with you so we can all talk together about your relationship.

There should be no surprise when a parishioner expresses reservations about accepting the pastor's invitation for both spouses to come together to the pastor's office. It is a common occurrence for a person to say, "Pastor, I would like to come with Gordon to talk with you, but three years ago we considered marriage counseling, and he said he would never see a marriage counselor even if it were free! I know he won't come. Once he makes up his mind, there's no changing him."

The pastor still does not know whether or not the parishioner's husband will come this time for couple counseling. All that is clear is that the wife is convinced he will not come. Either of two responses can be made.

Pastor: Your husband has been very reluctant in the past to have anything to do with marriage counseling. Please tell him I have invited both of you, because it is important for him to be involved with you for the improvement of your marriage.

Or the pastor may take the initiative:

Pastor: Your husband has some important reservations about coming
for marriage counseling. With your permission I will call him
and tell him you have talked with me about your concerns for
your marriage. And I will invite him to come with you to the
next session so the three of us can talk together about your
relationship.

Sometimes the second spouse will also request an individual session
with the pastor before coming together to see the pastor. The second
spouse can easily imagine that the pastor has heard only "bad things"
and therefore wants equal time with the pastor before the first session
of couple counseling. The pastor may have no option but to grant such
a request. In such preliminary individual sessions, marriage counseling
is not the primary goal for the pastor. The principal objective is to
communicate concern and understanding for both partners without
taking sides and then to offer once again the invitation for both of them
to come together to the pastor's office. In this first stage, the pastor's
main intention is to offer an invitation for them to sit down together
that both partners will accept.

A spouse may also turn down the pastor's invitation because of
confused or ambivalent feelings toward the marriage that need to be
clarified before couple counseling can even be considered. Ordinarily,
marriage counseling will not be productive if one partner has serious
reservations about continuing the marriage. Successful marriage counseling requires at least a basic commitment from both spouses that
they do want to be married to each other. When persons express
feelings of reservation or confusion about their commitment to the
marriage, the pastor can make one of two invitations to the husband
or wife.

Pastor: You are not at all sure you still love your wife, and you need
to think about your commitment to her before you can even
consider couple counseling. I'll be glad to help you sort through
those feelings. However, if more than two or three sessions are
needed for you individually, I will recommend that you and your
wife then go to another counselor for couple counseling. It
would not be fair to your wife for me first to become your
counselor and then attempt to be an unbiased counselor for
both of you as a couple.

Or the pastor may suggest the reverse plan.

Pastor: Because I am pastor for you both, I prefer to work with you
and your spouse from as unbiased a perspective as possible.

So I recommend that you do your individual counseling with another counselor, and when you are clearer about your feelings I will be more than glad to work with both of you in marriage counseling, if that is what you want.

It is important that a pastor not become confused about when and whether to do individual and couple counseling with one or both spouses. *As a rule, couple counseling and extended individual counseling with one or both spouses should not be done at the same time by the pastor. Nor should a pastor work with a couple if the pastor has done extended counseling earlier with one of the spouses. Unless both spouses feel the pastor is as much their own counselor as their partner's counselor, the success of the marriage counseling will be in jeopardy as soon as it begins.*

Some pastors may feel it is preferable to begin the marriage counseling by seeing both spouses separately from the outset. A case can be made that both partners may find it easier to talk to the pastor without the other being present, and it will be easier, presumably, for the pastor if the two spouses are not fighting with each other in the first session. However, the disadvantages of such a procedure ordinarily outweigh the advantages. Invariably, both husband and wife will be suspicious about what the pastor has been told individually before both come for counseling together. They each will be concerned that the pastor is going to be biased right from the beginning. For marriage counseling to have any chance of being helpful, it is usually necessary that both spouses know what the other has told the pastor about their marital differences. This, of course, requires that both spouses be present to hear what the other has to say. When that procedure occurs right from the beginning, neither spouse is as likely to think that the other has an unfair advantage. If either the husband or the wife begins to feel that the counseling process is unfair or that the pastor is no longer impartial, the counseling will have little hope of success.

Finally, if the pastor begins by seeing each partner separately for marriage counseling, it is more likely that the pastor will be seen as a judge who is to decide which spouse is right and which is wrong, having begun by hearing both partners' stories separately. It is not the pastor's job to be a judge, and the pastor cannot be an effective counselor if perceived to be in that role by either spouse. The pastor's intent to be equally concerned and unbiased toward both spouses is best ensured by inviting them to begin the marriage counseling process together.

The Initial Session with the Couple

In spite of the many details discussed in this book, the pastor who is beginning to use the brief marriage counseling model will do best to enter the first session trying to remember only the most general goals and principles from this chapter. Pastoral counseling has greater promise for being effective when it follows general guidelines in a natural manner instead of conforming minute by minute to the counselor's anxiously memorized expectations.

The setting. Unless circumstances require other arrangements, pastoral marriage counseling should usually occur in the pastor's office, not in the couple's home. Certainly, on some occasions it will be natural or even necessary for a pastor to do counseling with a couple in their living room or at their dining room table. It is possible for a pastor to accomplish much with a couple in their home surroundings. But in the pastor's office the pastor obviously has greater control over the physical arrangement of the furniture and can limit the possibility of any interruptions or intrusions. Marriage counseling is best done in a setting where privacy and confidentiality are ensured and where there is little likelihood of interruption at the door or on the telephone.

The purpose of pastoral marriage counseling is to facilitate a dialogue between husband and wife so that within the context of the Word their own words can take on new meaning for the renewal of their relationship. Pastoral marriage counseling also, by its very nature, must involve the pastor in that dialogue so that the candor and honesty of the pastor's words can encourage a truthful and open encounter between husband and wife. This encounter of words within the context and presence of the Word opens conflict and alienation once again to the possibility for reconciliation.

Such a theology of dialogic encounter for pastoral marriage counseling suggests a physical setting of three chairs arranged with no obstacle between them, so each person can see the other two with equal ease. There should not be a desk between the pastor and the couple, and it is usually better if the husband and wife are not seated side by side on a couch facing the pastor. If they are seated together on a couch, their own direct conversation, which is highly desirable, will be less natural, and they are more likely to talk to each other through the pastor instead of speaking directly to each other.

A box of tissues should be unobtrusively present. The absence of ashtrays indicates that no smoking is expected. A small clock may be set on a table in plain view of everyone, so the realistic limitations of time are always present. The pastor can say, "Let's do all we can in the next fifty minutes and then make plans for the next session." Such a comment at the beginning of the session will signal to the couple that there is a time to begin and a time to end, so everyone's attention can focus more promptly on the couple's main concerns and issues.

The pastor may wish to have a pad for recording notes during the session. Note-taking is certainly appropriate as long as it does not become an obvious block to communication or a distraction to the couple's concentration. If notes from counseling sessions are saved for future reference by the pastor, it is essential that some provision be made for keeping them in a securely locked file cabinet.

Goals and counselor responses. The pastor's hopes and expectations for the initial meeting with both spouses will remain in a proper perspective when the following goals and responses are kept in mind as guidelines.

1. *Provide a safe setting within which negative and destructive patterns of communication are interrupted.* An unfortunate fact of marital disharmony is that a basic trust has been lost, and both spouses no longer feel safe talking with their partner. Defensive and attacking language is characteristic of such marital crises, which prevents the couple from effectively communicating on their own to reach reconciliation and resolution. In the presence of a third person, their pastor, who represents authority and important faith values, both spouses should feel sufficient security so they can risk the kind of open discussion necessary for healing to begin in their marriage.

2. *Set ground rules to ensure communication in the counseling session that will encourage respectful and productive discussion.* Often, partners in the midst of serious conflict are not very kind or courteous toward each other. Such mutual disrespect heightens and intensifies defensiveness, making productive communication impossible. The pastor may set some ground rules in an explicit manner, such as asking that neither one interrupt the other but wait until each has finished talking before making a response. Often, essential ground rules for clear communication can be simply demonstrated if the pastor refuses to respond to an interrupting spouse and continues to direct attention to the spouse who is still talking. When one or both spouses interrupts the other or begins an argument, the pastor may say:

Pastor: I assume you both see some if not most issues quite differently from each other. It is important that both of you be able to speak without interruption so I can fully understand what each of you wants to say. It is best if you talk about yourself and your own feelings and refrain from describing or characterizing the other person.

By limiting the couple's references to each other as much as possible, the pastor makes it less likely that either spouse will feel the need to become defensive and argumentative during the first session.

3. *Enable both spouses to say in front of each other what they understand to be the problems and issues creating conflict in their marriage.* Healing dialogue is more likely to occur when the issues of conflict have been named out loud and each partner hears what is really troubling the other. The best way for the pastor to set the direction and tone of the counseling so the primary concerns can be identified is to open the first counseling session with a statement and then a question.

Pastor: (*Statement*) David, I talked with Shirley for about a half an hour last week, and she expressed some of her concerns for your marriage. I am glad you could both come tonight so we can talk together about the difficulties you both are experiencing at this time in your relationship. Now I need to hear from each of you how you see the issues or problems that are affecting your marriage.

(*Question*) What do you each feel is bringing you to counseling at this time, and what do you each want to accomplish here?

That question is central to the main purpose of the first session. For most of the time, the pastor will listen attentively as each spouse takes a turn answering that question. The pastor may find it particularly helpful to take careful notes, for the response given by each spouse will determine the direction of the counseling. Note-taking also signals to the couple that the pastor regards what they are saying as very important.

4. *Ascertain the current level of commitment of each spouse to the marriage and the counseling process.* The reason for this goal is twofold. If both spouses share a relatively high level of commitment to the marriage, knowledge of that commitment will motivate them to work earnestly toward the resolution of their conflicts. If, on the other hand, one or both of them have ambivalent or confused feelings about their level of commitment, it is essential for the sake of honesty that each spouse know exactly what the other's level of commitment really is. Nothing positive can be gained when one spouse falsely believes the counseling is for rebuilding the marriage when the other is about to file for divorce. Pastoral marriage counseling will have greater prospects for being helpful when both partners are honest with each other right from the start. About two thirds of the way through the first session, the pastor may feel it appropriate to raise this question.

Pastor: From what both of you have said here tonight, each of you has gone through a lot of pain and hurt over the years. Both of you have felt very misunderstood. Now I am wondering how much each of you really feels you still want to be married to the other. What about it, Roger? Do you still want to be married to Joyce?

Roger: That's a hard question to answer. You can be sure I've thought about it a lot. But I wouldn't be here tonight if I didn't want to stay married to her.

Pastor: Do you still love her?

Roger: Yes, I feel that I love her.

Pastor: Joyce, how about you? After all the conflict you and Roger have had between you, do you still want to be married to him?

Joyce: There have been many times when I gave up and thought I didn't want to remain in this marriage. But there is too much at stake, not only for Roger and me but also for the children. I'm not ready to turn my back on that.

Pastor: Do you feel you still love Roger?

Joyce: I'm mixed up about that right now. I'm not sure what love is anymore. But I'm not ready to give up on our marriage. I want to work with Roger to find a way so we can make it together, for our sakes and for the sake of our family.

Though this dialogue reflects the existence of much long-standing conflict in this marriage, there is some realistic basis for hope because both Roger and Joyce are committed to working toward improvement in their relationship.

5. *Communicate pastoral understanding and acceptance of both persons' views and feelings.* Pastoral understanding and acceptance are not to be confused with agreement by the pastor with either spouse. The test of whether the pastor has communicated basic understanding is whether both spouses feel that they have been heard and understood. When a person who is under much marital tension feels heard for the first time, the effect can be as dramatic as the lancing of a festering boil. Just the awareness that one has finally been listened to, even if by someone other than one's spouse, can begin an important healing process. In order to communicate such understanding, it is essential that the pastor avoid assuming not only the role of a judge, who will decide which spouse is right or wrong, but also the role of an expert, who has quick solutions on what should be done to "fix" a long-standing and deeply complicated marital conflict.

Most often the pastoral counselor will best communicate understanding to each spouse by using responses that accurately summarize the content and the feeling tone of what the person has been saying. In the following dialogue, Pastor Jean Barnes offers understanding responses to efforts by both Glenn and Sandra to make her into a judge and to elicit a quick-fix solution from her.

Glenn: I don't know how many times I've told Sandra to leave me alone for at least a half hour after I get home from work in the evening. After a full day of problems at the office and then fighting the wild drivers on the freeway, I need time to cool down, change my clothes, and relax with the newspaper. Don't you agree, Pastor, that anyone coming home after an exhausting day has a right to a few minutes to himself without having someone else's problems dumped on him?

Pastor: Glenn, you are feeling very frustrated because you have to deal with Sandra's concerns as soon as you get home from work. You're so worn out when you get home, you need to have some peaceful time to yourself so you can start to relax. You want Sandra to leave you alone for about thirty minutes before she begins to tell you about her own concerns.

Glenn: That's right. That's exactly how I feel!

Sandra: OK, but, what am I supposed to do? All day I live with screaming kids and a blaring TV. The first adult I've seen all day walks in the door, and I'm supposed to smile and say nothing while the kids are climbing all over me. Just tell me how I can do that and keep my sanity!

Pastor: Sandra, you are feeling at your wits' end by the end of the day, trying to cope with all the countless demands of small children. By the time Glenn comes in the door you are feeling desperate for communication with an adult who will give you some understanding and support.

Sandra: That's it exactly! Glenn just doesn't realize how important it is to me to sit down and share some of our deeper feelings with each other—like we did before we were married.

Pastor Barnes carefully avoided efforts to turn her into a judge to take Glenn's side or a giver of quick answers for Sandra. At this point, a solution offered by the pastor would most likely be rejected or discounted as not being good enough. The real issues, which Barnes affirmed by her responses, were the feelings and the content of the messages, which Glenn and Sandra needed to have someone hear. When Barnes was careful to respond in such a way that Glenn and Sandra really felt understood and heard, she also helped both Glenn and Sandra to be better understood and heard by each other.

6. *Make a preliminary pastoral assessment.* The brief marriage counseling model does not offer only one outcome. Rather, at any stage several options are always open, including termination or referral to other counseling resources. Before the pastor decides to invite the couple to continue counseling beyond the first session, other alternatives must be ruled out. For example, if one or both partners express very serious reservations about continuing the marriage at all, the pastor may choose to suggest that each do some individual counseling and then return for couple counseling when they are both certain that this is their common goal.

7. *Help a couple find some common ground on which they can begin to rebuild their distressed relationship.* When a couple comes for marriage counseling, all they can see is how fractured their relationship is. The pain of their differences looms up so large that it is virtually impossible for them to see what they ever had in common. The pastoral counselor tries to find at least one value, hope, experience, or commitment that the two partners share. Such a commitment may be a belief in the sanctity of their marriage or a determination to preserve their family life for the sake of their children. The pastor's discovery and *linking* of the couple's shared experiences or values can provide an essential starting point from which the couple can envision working together toward reconciliation.

Pastor Bill Walker linked Keith and Sarah through their remembrances of their courting days, their concern for their children, and the common pain they were both feeling in their marital conflicts.

Pastor: Sarah and Keith, the feelings you have expressed tonight make it clear that the conflict between you runs pretty deep. However, I heard you talking about the dreams you shared before your marriage. Also, it's clear that you both are very concerned about your two daughters and their futures. And though you find it hard to trust what the other says, I have no doubt from what I heard tonight that each of you, in your own way, is feeling very hurt and upset because of the tension in your relationship. I think you both agree a fresh start has to be made in nearly every area of your marriage.

Keith: Yes, I can believe this is as hard on Sarah as it is on me. Sarah, I can work with you on this if we can both agree to change almost everything. I know we just can't go on the way we have been!

Sarah: We have a long way to go before we can ever reclaim any of those dreams we had when we first met. But I'll work with you on our marriage, Keith, if you are really committed to putting your heart into it this time.

By finding ways to join Keith and Sarah together, even in the similarity of their personal pain and anguish, Pastor Walker helped this couple find some common ground where they could begin talking and working toward reconciliation.

Throughout the marriage counseling process, the pastor should always be looking for legitimate ways *to link the couple* by drawing their attention to experiences, views, or feelings they hold in common, even if they are negative experiences or feelings. Such linking may in some cases bring a husband and wife to see that they have more in common than the painful differences absorbing so much of their attention. Any attempts to link a couple should not be done in such a way as to imply that their differences are insignificant or not to be taken seriously. But drawing attention to significant concerns or feelings that both spouses have in common may set their differences in such a context that they will see new possibilities for resolving the conflicts that are separating them.

8. *Offer realistic hope and a promising strategy for the couple to deal with their problems.* Realistic hope never minimizes the severity of conflict, while it envisions the best that is possible. A wise pastor will resist any urge to be overly reassuring. Most couples come to counseling with the knowledge that they are dealing with serious problems in their marriage. If the pastor suggests that the problems are not as serious as the couple sees them, the couple may rightly assume that their pastor has not really understood the full depth of their feelings.

The best basis for any hope is the willingness on the part of each spouse to work with the other toward reconciliation. When such willingness is present, the pastor can, with confidence, suggest that the outline of the brief counseling model be followed. If the couple accepts the pastor's recommendation, the pastor will give each of them a copy of the Pastoral Marriage Counseling Questionnaire and make plans to see each spouse individually. Pastor Wayne Knoll decided that the best way to proceed with Bruce and Laura was to suggest the outline for brief marriage counseling.

Pastor: Laura and Bruce, I am glad we had the opportunity tonight to talk about these problems that you both have been wrestling with for such a long time. They are not simple problems, obviously, or you would have found a solution for them years ago. You both have been hurt, and I am not surprised each of you has given thought to whether divorce is the only way out. But tonight I have not heard either one of you saying you are ready to quit. And even though you are very upset, you both still have a basic respect and appreciation for the other. If there were a way for things to be worked out, you both said you still want to be married. That offers some hope that you have a place to start rebuilding for the future of your marriage and your family.

Here is the best way I can help you. I want to propose a plan for a specific number of counseling sessions over the next four to six weeks. At the end of that period we can reassess what progress has been made and what should be the next step. The counseling sessions would follow this pattern: I would give each of you a questionnaire to take home with you tonight. Your answers to the questions would give me more detailed information and also help you reflect about yourselves and your marriage and put those thoughts on paper. Next, I would meet with each of you separately for one or perhaps two individual sessions, but no more than two sessions alone. I would need you to return the completed questionnaires to me two days before the first individual session so I would have time to read them through before we meet. I would return the questionnaires to you after the counseling process is completed.

Then, following the individual sessions, I would see the two of you together two times. At the last session, we would take a careful look at the progress you have made and evaluate what still needs to be done for the lasting changes you both want for your marriage. The sessions should be about a week apart, though I could see both of you individually next week if you wish.

I do not have ready answers or solutions for the problems that have been troubling both of you for so long. But I do care very much about both of you. The plan I am suggesting will give you both time for learning more about yourselves, about each other, and about what goes on between the two of you that causes so much misunderstanding. The strategy I am proposing does not offer a guarantee, but through the process both of you will be able to make better decisions about what you are willing to do for the future of your marriage and the sake of your family.

Laura: I knew our problems were too big for us to solve tonight, though I suppose I was hoping, Pastor, that you might have a magic wand that would fix everything and take away the pain. Your suggestion is realistic, and it gives us something concrete to work on. I'm willing if you are, Bruce.

Bruce: Well, I suppose I too had hoped for a quick fix, but I should have known better. At least in a couple of weeks we should know more than we know now, and maybe the extra time will give us a little better perspective. Yes, Pastor, let's go ahead. Do we get the questionnaire now that you were talking about?

Pastor: Yes. And one more thing. I want to ask that you not read each other's completed questionnaire. That is my rule. Your responses are only for me to read.

9. Set the counseling within the context of God's care for both spouses despite the uncertainties in their relationship and their unanswered questions. The pastor always enters every counseling relationship with a sense of prayer that seeks God's grace and guidance for the couple. In the course of the first session the pastor may find appropriate and natural occasions for talking about the reality of God's presence and love, doing so in such a manner that the couple can still feel open about expressing negative and conflicted feelings about their marriage and about their faith. When going through upheaval in one's marriage, one may naturally question God's concern and whether God takes seriously prayers for help and guidance. The pastor, through the use of faith language, prayer, and scripture, will want to be careful and sensitive about offering a witness to God's grace and purpose that will be experienced by both spouses as affirming and reassuring.

Conclusion

It should not be the pastor's purpose to try to solve the couple's marital conflicts in the first session, with both the husband and the wife. Such an expectation is totally unrealistic for nearly all couples who find their way to the pastor's office. Within a structured setting, the pastor's aims for the first session are (1) to permit both persons to tell their spouse and the pastor exactly how they see the problems in the marriage, (2) to convey understanding to both spouses, (3) to offer realistic hope, and (4) to outline a plan for proceeding with further counseling sessions. By keeping these goals in mind, and not trying to fix all the couple's problems in the first meeting, the pastor should feel much less anxiety about the initial session and, in fact, will accomplish much for the couple if those limited goals can be attained.

The pastor's main intent should be to help both spouses make their own best decisions about the future of the marriage. Charles Stewart has emphasized that the pastor avoid advice-giving and, instead, is "*for* the individuals, for their right to choose their own destiny under God, and for the possibility of there coming creative solutions out of dis-creative situations."[4] With that hope of finding creative alternatives to a broken relationship, the pastor is now ready to prepare for counseling sessions with each spouse individually.

3

INDIVIDUAL SESSIONS
WITH EACH SPOUSE

It is almost like saying that the more separate you become, the greater is the chance for a strong union. . . . A living partnership is composed of two people, each of whom owns, respects, and develops his or her own selfhood.

—Carl R. Rogers[1]

The separate meetings with husband and wife will require preparation on the part of the pastor. At the initial session, when the Pastoral Marriage Counseling Questionnaire was given to each person, the pastor asked that the questionnaires be completed and returned two days before the individual counseling sessions. Also, it is important for the pastor to request that the couple not share their responses to the questionnaire with each other. Such a guideline ensures that each person will feel free to answer the questions candidly.

Analysis and Use of the Pastoral
Marriage Counseling Questionnaire

The purpose of the Pastoral Marriage Counseling Questionnaire is twofold. First, the information requested will help the pastor consider the wide range of factors that can contribute to marital conflict and thus see more of the whole picture, beyond the specific complaints presented by the husband and the wife. Second, the process of responding to the questionnaire can help many persons gain new and helpful understandings about themselves and their marriage. The pastor and the couple will all be able to make better use of the individual counseling sessions after the questionnaires have been completed and returned.

The Pastoral Marriage Counseling Questionnaire should be considered as a model that can be revised or altered to suit each pastor's needs. However, the questionnaire in its present form is designed to secure information essential for most marriage counseling circumstances.

Specific marital problems can ordinarily be best understood when they are viewed in the context of the total marriage, and in fact in the context of the present and former life experiences of both partners. The questions provide preliminary information in the areas of people's experience that can most directly affect a marriage positively or negatively.

Pastors should read their parishioners' responses to the questionnaire with both an inquiring and an understanding eye. Certainly, more experienced counselors will bring greater understanding and perception to the responses supplied by their parishioners. The beginning counselor should be reassured to know that even professional counselors would arrive at differing conclusions from the materials found in returned questionnaires. So every pastor should take a relaxed attitude about what parishioners write and not try too hard to arrive at elaborate interpretations of the data.

The pastor should return the questionnaires to the couple when the counseling process is completed. Therefore, it is probably wise not to make notes on the questionnaires. Even check marks or circled items can later distract counselees from the results of the counseling. And during the time a completed questionnaire remains in the pastor's possession, *it is essential that all possible security measures be taken to ensure that the questionnaire will not be read by another person without the counselee's permission.*

The following discussion of items on the questionnaire will offer the pastor guidelines for identifying issues that might be important for further exploration in individual sessions with each spouse. *It should always be remembered as the questionnaire is analyzed that the pastor's role, in nearly every instance, is not to be a judge rendering a verdict as to which spouse is right or wrong, but, rather, to gain the fullest understanding possible of the conflicted pattern of the relationship between the two partners.*

Courtship and Marriage

1. How did you and your spouse first meet? Every couple has a different story to tell about the first meeting. The circumstances of that initial encounter are obviously essential to understanding the couple's marriage and the development of their relationship. For some couples, it can be very helpful to review with them how they first met and the hopes they had as their courtship began to develop.

2. What were your reasons for marrying your spouse? Seriously conflicted marriages often reflect early decisions that got the marriage off to a questionable start right from the outset. In some difficult situations, spouses acknowledge that they really did not, nor do they now, want to be married to their partner. Very hard decisions for both spouses usually have to be made following such a realization. On the other hand, some couples have been able to salvage an ill-conceived relationship and, through much pain and hard work, have built an enduring marriage despite the questionable motives they had when they first decided to marry.

3. What was your honeymoon like, and what were your feelings about it? Responses to this question can offer important clues about the beginning of a marriage. If one partner says that the honeymoon was great, and the other spouse recalls that the honeymoon was a miserable experience, one may rightly wonder if their communication problems may date from day one of their marriage. A couple who agrees that their honeymoon was essentially a happy experience may find it helpful in their current stage of conflict to remember the early positive beginnings of their marriage. And if a couple is unanimous in agreeing that their honeymoon was an unhappy time, this may be a clear indication that the marriage never enjoyed a solid beginning or foundation.

4. Do you have any children? If yes, give their names, ages, and school grades. If a couple does not have children, it may be informative for the pastor to inquire how that decision was made. It may, in fact, have not been a decision but rather the result of unsuccessful attempts to become pregnant. Or one partner may have made the decision, with the other spouse reluctantly concurring while inwardly longing someday to be a parent. Did the childless couple consider adoption, and how was that decision made? The answers to these questions may offer important insights into the communication pattern between husband and wife.

A pastor should always bear in mind that the arrival of each child makes new, stressful demands on the marriage. Although husbands often feel replaced by the first child, it is not extraordinary for a mother to feel jealous if the first child shows a preference for the father. A pastor will often gain important information about a marriage by inquiring, "What changes do you recall occurred in your marriage with the arrival of each of your children? And how were you particularly affected by those changes?"

The number of children and the range of their ages will offer indications about the kinds of parenting tasks facing the couple. Couples with two infant children under eighteen months of age have a different set of problems from a couple with two children in college at the same time. And the parents of two or three adolescent children are often dealing with concerns that can challenge the most harmonious marriage

5. Where do children outside the home live? After children leave home, they remain a matter of much concern and even stress for many couples. One husband told the counselor, "Our twenty-three-year-old son is somewhere downtown, but we do not know where he is living. We haven't heard from him for seven months. We just hope he's OK. He'll probably show up when he is broke and ask us to take him in. We get into arguments about it, because his mother thinks I was too hard on him, making him leave home before he was ready to be on his own. But I tell her, 'After all, he is twenty-three!' "

Do most of the children live within a fifty-mile radius of their parents' home? If they do, does that mean they often return home? Are family reunions or gatherings with children important? Older couples may find helpful support and encouragement when their children live nearby and there is frequent interaction. This will especially be the case in situations where good relationships exist between the parents and their children. It is important that the pastor, when assessing where the children live, note also the quality of the relationships between the parents and their children and the impact of those relationships upon the parents' marriage.

6. If any children are no longer living, when and how did they die? The death of a child, no matter at what age, is a profound trauma for parents to experience. Such a death may mark a turning point of major proportions in the marriage. Such a crisis has the potential for either drawing a couple closer together or causing recurring tensions and conflicts.

Even the death of an unborn child can represent a loss as severe to many couples as the death of any other child. One husband regularly gives his wife flowers on Mother's Day, even though she has had three unsuccessful pregnancies. Their relationship has grown stronger as they have faced the disappointment of having no children.

Suicide is the number-two cause of death among youth in this country.[2] Couples may also lose a child through illness or an automobile accident. When such a loss has occurred, the pastor should inquire how the parents adjusted to it. The loss of a child should be explored carefully, because it will usually represent a critical transition that may contribute significantly to current tensions and conflicts in the marriage.

7. Have you or your spouse been married before? If so, when and how did that marriage end? The pastor wants to find out whether an earlier marriage is possibly continuing to affect the present one. In some cases, this is an especially pertinent question when one of the spouses entered the present marriage before resolving feelings about the ending of the former marriage. Is there still unresolved grief about the death of one's first wife or husband? Did one partner remarry too soon after a divorce?

Former marriages always influence a subsequent marriage. Is the former marriage a contributing source of the current tension and conflict? Is there any evidence that a formerly married person has learned from mistakes or poor judgments that were made in the earlier marriage? Or has there been little personal growth, so the person can be expected to make similar mistakes in the present marriage?

8. Do the current problems in your marriage include any of the following? This section of the questionnaire helps pinpoint specific complaints and concerns about the marriage.

a. Lack of communication. In some manner, all marital conflicts can be attributed to troubled patterns of communication. The busy pace of modern life can easily be used by many couples as an excuse for withdrawing from each other during times of tension and misunderstanding. Preoccupation with the children or with one's professional life can make it easy to justify behaviors that distance one from one's spouse. Most couples do not have the skills to interrupt their deteriorating interactions when one or both of them feels hurt by something the other has said or done. Ordinarily, instead of taking action to reverse the hurtful communications, couples will resort to angry outbursts or sarcastic and cynical remarks that deepen the hurt.

b. Sexual or physical abuse. The husband will be the abuser in most instances, but not always. Many victims of physical or sexual abuse often find it difficult to report or discuss the abusive behavior of a partner. The purpose of this question is to make it possible for the topic to be discussed in the counseling process.

Some people used to think that if a woman was being abused she had somehow asked for it. Such thinking is similar to the notion that if a woman is raped she somehow asked to be raped. *There is never any justification for either person, wife or husband, to be sexually or physically abused.* Nonetheless, it can be very shaming for one or both partners to acknowledge to their pastor that abuse is a factor in the problems they are trying to resolve. A more detailed discussion of how the pastor may deal with instances of abuse appears in chapter 5. Under any circumstances, quickly made reassurances that "I won't hit her again" need very careful evaluation.

c. Infidelity. No marriage that is fulfilling for both spouses can long survive once the basic trust between them has been violated. In most marriages, the most damaging violation of that trust occurs when one partner has an affair. An affair may never be found out by the other partner, and so remains a secret never revealed. If the affair does come to light, it will ordinarily create a marital crisis of enormous proportions; in some cases the offended spouse finally seeks a divorce. On the other hand, some couples are able to go through an intense period of reconciliation, and sufficient trust can be restored for the marriage to continue.

Sometimes a spouse who has had an affair feels sufficient guilt to consider telling his or her partner about it. It is usually highly questionable whether revealing the secret will help the marital relationship. Of course, the guilty spouse will need to make up his or her own mind. A pastor can be a valuable resource in such a situation, assisting the person to consider in a careful manner all the pros and cons of disclosing the extramarital involvement.

Marriage counseling cannot be done if one of the spouses is currently engaged in a romantic or sexual relationship outside the marriage. Some persons will come to marriage counseling as a way of testing which relationship matters more to them, their marriage or the extramarital attraction. *Marriage counseling cannot be effective unless the marriage is the primary relationship for both partners and both are committed to growth in their marriage and to the counseling process!* Consequently, to proceed with marriage counseling when one of the spouses is having an affair is to invite frustration and disappointment when the counseling fails to produce resolution and renewed commitment within the marriage.

Also, pastors can no longer ignore the possibility that the spouse involved in an extramarital sexual liaison may unknowingly be a carrier of the AIDS (Acquired Immune Deficiency Syndrome) virus. In every situation the circumstances will be different, but the pastor will need to consider both spouses' and pastor's ethical responsibilities for informing the unknowing partner about the possibility of exposure to AIDS.

d. In-law involvement. A satisfactory marriage requires that each spouse feel the other's first loyalty is to the marriage and not one's parents. In a good marriage, the bond between husband and wife is stronger than any other family relationship. When scripture says that a man shall leave his father and mother in order to live solely with his wife (Gen. 2:24), the point is clear that a new set of boundaries has been drawn for the sake of the marriage and the resulting family.

Well-meaning but destructive intrusion by in-laws can happen in any family. Bonnie put down the telephone and turned angrily toward Gary. "That was your mother, and she's complaining again that we never visit them on holidays with the kids. I've had it, Gary. We've been to their house every Christmas and every Thanksgiving for the past four years. It's time your parents realized we have to have our own family life!"

In-laws can overstep a couple's boundaries in countless ways, and a husband and wife may often feel guilty about confronting excessive claims on their marital and family time and energy. A pastor can assist by helping the couple to see more clearly the boundaries they need to observe and protect for the sake of the primacy of their own relationship.

e. Finances. Disagreements over the management of money is a major source of conflict for many couples, and resolving differences in this area is all the more difficult when basic patterns for effective communication have deteriorated.

Financial stress exists for couples in every income bracket. Moreover, conflicts over how to spend money often reflect basic differences over values. Connie exclaimed about Don's purchase of a large boat. "He just bought that boat for show. I think it's dumb! We need to remodel the kitchen far more than we need such an outrageously expensive boat. But, do you think he listens to me? Of course not!" A pastor can be of considerable help in exploring the basic values that underlie a couple's different spending patterns.[3]

f. Problems relating to children. Being a parent is not an easy responsibility, and what seems to work with one child can have quite the opposite effect with another child. Moreover, both parents quite naturally bring differing experiences and backgrounds from their former families as they make decisions about their children. Even effective, mature, wise parents do not always agree on how to bring up their children. Indeed, it ordinarily is to the children's benefit when their parents bring broad and varying perspectives to the parenting task. As a result, the primary challenge for the parents is to listen to each other and to negotiate policies for child-rearing that reflect the essential views and feelings of both partners.

Most couples will agree that if they are communicating effectively with each other they can manage to handle the crises that are to be expected with each child. The pastor will be a significant help by assisting couples to strengthen their own bonding and mutual understanding as they try to make the best decisions for their children.

g. Work-related problems. Most married persons spend more waking time each day at work than they do at home. Many of the frustrations at work will be felt somehow by one's spouse. When people are overwhelmed by work tensions they may withdraw. The spouse senses something is wrong but cannot be sure what it is.

When work problems are creating anxiety in a person, another common pattern is to resort to increased hours on the job, which results in even fewer hours at home with one's partner. So-called workaholism is rationalized by many spouses as simply a fact of life that has to be tolerated so their partner can have a successful career and bring home a more desirable paycheck. But some spouses do not like to pay the price of spending several nights a week by themselves for the sake of a partner's career. Nor are husbands the only offenders!

Bob went to his minister to say he could no longer put up with his wife's obsession with her work. She would wake up at 4:00 A.M. in order to be in the office an hour and a half before her colleagues and get a head start on them for the day. Bob wanted his wife back, and the minister's counseling with Bob and his wife included discussing how she could keep her work hours within more reasonable limits.

Pastors must remember that work within the home can be as demanding as work outside the home. Also, clergy (clergymen in particular) should be sensitive to how most women who work outside the home still feel responsible for all the chores and responsibilities at home. Consequently, most women workers feel they have two jobs: their nine-to-five one and their traditional homemaking. The sensitive pastoral counselor will attend to how husbands and wives are negotiating and sharing household responsibilities when both go out to work.

h. Alcohol or chemical abuse. Alcohol or chemical abuse is always disruptive, in a marriage and in the family. Sharon Wegscheider has described the various roles that are played by family members where there is alcohol or chemical abuse.[4] The counseling pastor does well to become familiar with Wegscheider's description of the family dynamics that develop in order to cope with the crisis of chemical abuse. Most often, the spouse of the alcoholic takes the role of enabler. In that role, the spouse invariably supports the chemical abuse despite the pain and emotional turmoil it causes. The enabler usually makes excuses for the drinking spouse's behavior and in other subtle ways supports the abusing spouse's pattern of chemical dependence.

A pastor has many judgment decisions to make in those cases where chemical abuse is part of the marital conflict. Should steps be taken to get the chemically dependent person into treatment? Consultation with a chemical dependency treatment facility should help the spouse or family and the pastor decide whether to make plans for a possible confrontation and intervention that will lead the abusing spouse into treatment.

Another important question is whether it is worth the time and effort to attempt any marriage counseling at all if the chemically dependent spouse goes untreated or continues to use alcohol or other chemicals. As those questions are being evaluated, the pastor must also decide how direct to be with both spouses about the chemical abuse and its effect on the marriage. In most instances, a straightforward approach is more effective than failing to identify the chemical abuse as a destructive factor in the marriage. Though the spouse who is accused of abusing alcohol or other chemicals may deny that such abuse is occurring, the fact that the other spouse is troubled about the behavior makes the matter an important issue for the marriage counseling process.

i. Sexual adjustment problems. Even in the best of marriages, the communication and satisfaction of sexual needs is always a complex and delicate interaction. The process becomes immensely complicated when each partner naturally assumes that sexual intimacy for one's spouse is experienced in the same way as one's own sexuality. This erroneous assumption often leads to much marital misunderstanding, frustration, and hurt. Chapter 5 presents a more detailed discussion of marital sexual problems.

In many instances, complaints about sexual problems may be symptomatic of a more basic intimacy problem for the couple. Satisfying intimacy in most aspects of the marriage is usually a basic prerequisite if a couple is to have a rewarding sexual relationship. The primary role of intimacy for a husband and wife has been emphasized in the book *Masters and Johnson on Sex and Human Loving.* Far from offering only a discussion of the biology and the mechanics of human sexuality, the book also focuses on the fundamental role of intimacy in chapter 10, entitled "Intimacy and Communication Skills." As the author points out,

> Intimacy can be defined as a process in which two caring people share as freely as possible in the exchange of feelings, thoughts, and actions.... Intimacy is generally marked by a mutual sense of acceptance, commitment, tenderness, and trust.[5]

A primary task for every marriage is for the couple to negotiate with each other how they can best meet each other's needs for intimacy and sexual expression in ways that are comfortable for both partners. This negotiation does not occur just one time within the first three weeks of marriage. It is a continuing process of negotiation throughout the marriage. And this essential communication can be successful only if it is based on the kind of sensitivity and understanding on both sides reflected in the statement just quoted.

Effective pastoral marriage counseling will help to facilitate the growth of renewed levels of intimacy. It is not at all unusual for couples to report that their sexual relationship has improved as they have made significant strides toward intimate sharing in other areas of their marriage. Pastors will help many couples improve their sexual relationship without ever even discussing sex, the improvement coming as the counseling focuses on new ways for changing conflicted intimacy and communication patterns.

j. Unfulfilled emotional needs. As a pastor listens to troubled couples, reported unfulfilled emotional needs will become apparent in any of three areas. One area will relate to the extent to which both spouses feel they are the *primary commitment* in the other's life. For most married persons, their marriage is not fully satisfying if they feel they are only one among many of their partner's commitments. The emotional expectation for most persons is that they will be more important to their partner than any other person, object, or relationship. Moreover, it is essential for a happy marriage that the primary importance of one's spouse be repeatedly and continually communicated in ways the other readily understands. Saying "I love you" every morning does not have a great deal of meaning after coming home late four nights in a row with a time-worn excuse, "I had a lot to do at the office." There are very few husbands and wives who do not have the basic emotional need to be first in their partners' lives.

The second basic emotional need for married persons is *trust.* Trust that undergirds the mutually satisfying marriage encompasses several dimensions of the relationship. Both partners need to know they can trust the other person in relationships with other people. Regardless of the nature of those relationships, both spouses need to feel that their marital relationship will remain inviolate as the primary commitment for each. Also, when both spouses are in each other's presence, they need to know that they can trust the other, that they will be safe both physically and psychically. Such trust permits spouses to be emotionally and intimately vulnerable to each other without fearing that they will be "beat up" or "beat on," either physically, sexually, or verbally.

The third main area of emotional need in secure marriages is best identified as *companionship.* Husbands and wives have important emotional needs satisfied when they can problem-solve together and play together. Companionship in marriage includes making hard decisions for the sake of the children, going for a walk together on a Sunday night, or cleaning the house together. Companionship is important because it fulfills that emotional need all married people have for knowing their partner wants to be with them and enjoys spending time with them. When companionship is missing, a marriage will fail to satisfy basic emotional needs in both spouses.

k. Lack of spiritual growth. Many husbands and wives value highly the encouragement they receive from their partner for growth in their faith and spiritual life. Many couples, in fact, were originally drawn together through common concerns and interests about the church and their faith. As the pastor inquires into this important area of the marriage, it will not be unusual to hear couples expressing concern that they no longer pray together or find time to maintain the devotional life together that formerly meant so much to their relationship.

Keeping a vital connection with one's spiritual center is essential for all persons. And just as each individual's spiritual journey takes unique paths and directions, so couples will find many different ways for supporting each other toward growth in their faith. Some couples may report that they do not often talk about their faith but feel a spiritual closeness that is reassuring. Other couples may prefer a regular devotional pattern that includes reading scripture and praying together. The sensitive pastor will encourage each couple to follow patterns that are comfortable and growth-enhancing, and not discouraging or guilt-producing. If couples gain the impression that unless they follow a prescribed routine they cannot be growing Christians, they may easily become disheartened about their spiritual life together. However, if a pastor can affirm whatever practices a couple reports are spiritually enlivening for them, they will feel encouraging support for their spiritual intimacy and growth together.

9–11. Who is going to make changes? It is important for the pastor to keep in mind two essential questions, which can be addressed either individually or in the joint sessions with both husband and wife present. First, what changes in general need to occur so the marriage can undergo a significant change for the better? Second, what changes are you yourself willing to make so there can be greater harmony in the marriage?

Asking a couple to consider these questions can help them move beyond their complaints about the past to focus on what can be done better in the future. Experienced pastoral counselors know that the first question can often elicit much faultfinding of the other spouse. For example:

Pastor: Carol, what do you think needs to happen in your marriage so there will be less tension between you and Dwight?

Carol: Dwight is so uncommunicative! I need someone to talk to. I got married so I could share my feelings and hopes with another person. When Dwight comes home from work I ask him how his day has gone, and all I get is a grunt and a snort. Dwight needs to learn how to communicate.

The pastor knows that Carol's attitude will need to change before much will begin to change in the marriage. Even though Dwight may not be very communicative, it is important for Carol to recognize her own part in the blocking that occurs between them. A more promising response to the pastor's question might be:

Carol: Dwight is so uncommunicative! Because I'm so glad to see him, I guess I start talking as soon as he gets in the door, almost before he can take his coat off and catch his breath. For our marriage to get back on the right track, we probably need to find a better time for talking with each other that fits well for both our schedules and our personal preferences.

Such a response shows that Carol has moved beyond blaming to a posture of looking for ways that she and Dwight can work together to resolve the sources of their conflicts. Hearing such a constructive response, the pastor can rightly conclude that there is hope for the couple's making good progress toward improving their relationship.

The question that gets to the heart of the matter is what each spouse is prepared to change about his or her own behavior in order to reduce the marital conflict. Before asking this question, the pastor should realize that all persons have limits to how far they will go toward making concessions or changes in a troubled relationship. It can even be helpful for the pastor to make that observation out loud. Moreover, it is essential to realize that neither pastor nor spouse can make another person change. Most persons will make changes when they see that such changes are basically in their own best interests. And having a harmonious marriage with far less conflict can, for many people, be strongly motivating.

The pastor may address this issue in this manner:

Pastor: Dwight, you have been telling me many things about Carol that have made you unhappy. Like many persons who come to marriage counseling, you may even have consented to come here with Carol in hopes that I would get her to change some of her ways that are so irritating for you. But you and I cannot change Carol. Rather, I must ask you if you have considered what you yourself are prepared to change within you or in your responses to Carol. I assume that there are things you would not consider changing, but what are you willing to change for the sake of your marriage?

Dwight: I wondered if you would ask me that question. Of course, it is easier for me to see what Carol needs to change. Sometimes it feels like she wants me to be someone different from who I really am. I know I'm not the world's greatest conversationalist. But I suppose I should give Carol more time. Maybe we could take a walk together in the evening after supper, or something like that. I'm usually beat right after work when I get home, but if I start working with Carol in the kitchen after supper, we could take a twenty-minute walk after the food and dishes are cleared up.

The pastoral counselor can facilitate significant change in a conflicted marriage by encouraging and supporting specific change such as Dwight says he is willing to make. Unfortunately, in many troubled marriages so much bitterness prevails that neither partner is willing to make a positive change until the other partner acts first. Conflict leads to an impasse, as each spouse tries to outwait the other rather than take steps to meet halfway. The pastor will see encouraging progress taking place as soon as one or both spouses follows through on the changes they themselves are willing to make.

Family of Origin

The pastoral counselor's evaluation of the marriage needs to take account of the family histories for both husband and wife. The experiences and relationships people have in their early formative years are very influential in the development of adult patterns of behavior. As the pastor inquires about personal family history, important clues may emerge that will be of help to the individual as well as to the pastor.

Particularly significant is how one recalls the relationship between his or her parents. It is not unusual to hear people make the observation that they never saw their parents kiss or hug each other or exchange any expression of affection. For these people, such a parental model can prove inhibiting as they try to express affection toward their own partner.

Relationships with one's own parents, and particularly the parent of the opposite gender, can also be an influence in one's own marriage. The man who was used to having his mother take care of all his needs as a child may still expect his wife to wake him up in the morning and lay out his clothes for work. Or a woman who was fearful of her father may find it difficult to develop the trust with her husband necessary for true intimacy.

The role people have played in their family of origin may shed light on their responses to current marital crises. The person who was the oldest child, responsible for the other children and perhaps for quite a few household chores, may respond to marital problems by taking charge and becoming more controlling. A child who played the martyr, letting others dump responsibility on him or her, may follow a similarly passive martyr role in the marriage, while feeling very angry inside about being in that position.

It is essential that the pastor know whether there is any history of physical, sexual, or chemical abuse in a person's family of origin. Questions 19 and 20 of the Pastoral Marriage Counseling Questionnaire offer the opportunity to respond to these questions. Chemical or alcohol abuse in one's family history is always a significant influence on the patterns and behaviors adopted in adult years.

Janet Woititz's generalizations are based on her work with adults who grew up with alcohol abuse in their home. According to Woititz, adult children of alcoholics:

- Guess at what normal behavior is.
- Have difficulty following a project through from beginning to end.
- Lie when it would be just as easy to tell the truth.
- Judge themselves without mercy.
- Have difficulty having fun.
- Take themselves very seriously.
- Have difficulty with intimate relationships.
- Overreact to changes over which they have no control.
- Constantly seek approval and affirmation.
- Usually feel they are different from other people.
- Are super responsible or super irresponsible.
- Are extremely loyal even in the face of evidence that the loyalty is undeserved.
- Are impulsive, tending to lock themselves into a course of action without giving serious consideration to alternative behaviors or possible consequences. This impulsiveness leads to confusion, self-loathing, and loss of control over their environment. In addition, they spend an excessive amount of energy cleaning up the mess.[6]

Woititz also observes that professionals who treat alcoholics generally agree that alcoholism runs in families, that children of alcoholics are more likely to develop alcoholism than others, and that children of alcoholics are more likely to marry an alcoholic person.[7]

Woititz's generalizations will not apply equally to all adult children of alcoholics. However, her findings offer important guidelines for the pastoral counselor to use for evaluating marriages where chemical abuse is part of the family history.

Pastors should always be sensitive to the fact that both past and present experiences of physical or sexual abuse are very difficult for most persons to discuss with their pastor. It may be especially difficult for a parishioner to discuss sexual matters with a pastor of the opposite sex. There also may be much reluctance to discuss past or present experiences of abuse out of fear that one will not be believed or that one's partner will retaliate. Pastoral options for responses to domestic abuse or violence are discussed in chapter 5.

One's personal history does not have to doom one to a life of unsatisfactory intimate relationships. As human beings, we always have opportunities to make new choices about how we will respond to life's daily options. However, painful experiences early in one's life can continue to block efforts by both spouses to improve their relationship. A pastor asked a woman if at any time in her life she had ever had any thoughts, feelings, or experiences that had been disturbing. At first she did not mention any, but then her eyes began to fill with tears as she described being five years old and hearing through her parents' bedroom door her father sexually abusing her mother. She exclaimed, "That memory has never left me! I think about it when Larry and I are trying to make love, and it just takes all my feeling away!" The sensitive pastor will listen very carefully, for the personal history of each spouse is a continuing major influence upon the marital problems the couple needs to resolve.

The Counseling Process for Meeting with Each Spouse

The pastor increases the possibility for the individual counseling sessions to be productive by making careful preparations for those meetings. The counseling process with each spouse has three phases. The first is the reading and analysis of the responses to the Pastoral Marriage Counseling Questionnaire, the next is preparation of an outline for the actual individual sessions, and the third phase is one of reflection and reaching tentative conclusions following each individual session.

Analyzing the questionnaire. The pastor is not expected to function as a sophisticated psychologist when reading the completed questionnaires. Pastors will bring their own wisdom and insights based on their training, personal life experiences, familiarity with the couple being counseled, and pastoral commitment to being a part of God's helping process. It is appropriate for the pastor to trust that he or she is making the best possible judgments in assessing the questionnaires. Consultation with another professional person regarding the questionnaire may also be a helpful option for the pastor.

The primary goal, when assessing information provided by parishioners, should be one of *seeking understanding,* not determining blame. The intention of increasing understanding provides the most helpful context for each spouse. As the pastor asks questions for understanding, the counselee should begin to gain greater self-understanding and further insight into the marital conflicts.

Preparing an outline. The following format is recommended for the first individual session with each spouse:

1. The pastor will open the session by explaining the purpose for the next fifty minutes. The stated objective is to explore the broader aspects of the marital conflicts and to offer the opportunity for the spouse to discuss any personal concerns privately with the pastor. The pastor can add appreciation for the effort made in completing the questionnaire and also ask what the experience was like. It can be important for the individual to have an opportunity to express either satisfaction or frustration with the questionnaire.

2. Next, the pastor may ask how things are in the marriage at the moment. This question helps the pastor learn of any changes that may have occurred since the last counseling session. Comparing the individual answers of husband and wife to this question can give the pastor important clues about their views of the marriage. If the husband thinks there is very little tension at the moment, but the wife reports that matters are worse than ever because her husband is coming home less, the pastor has learned important information for assessing the depth of the conflict.

The question about "how things are" will also help the pastor learn if any significant changes have occurred in the couple's living arrangements. It is important to know if either spouse has moved out or if they have decided to end a period of separation and are now living together again.

3. Sometime during the individual session it is important that the pastor inquire if the counselee is now or has ever been involved in an affair. If should not be assumed that this information will be volunteered without the question being asked. And some persons may not answer truthfully, not wanting their pastor to know about an adulterous relationship. However, if an extramarital relationship is a factor, the pastor must make careful judgments about the continuing focus and direction of the marital counseling process.

The inquiry about an extramarital relationship may be made in the context of asking how long the couple has been married and whether it is a first or subsequent marriage for either of them.

Pastor: Carrie, how long have you and Greg been married?
Carrie: We have been married sixteen years, as of last May.
Pastor: Is this the first marriage for each of you?
Carrie: No. I was married once before.

Pastor: How and when did that marriage end?

Carrie: Tim was killed in an automobile accident a year and a half before I met Greg.

Pastor: In the sixteen years you and Greg have been married, have you ever had any relationship with anyone outside your marriage?

Carrie: No.

Pastor: In that time have you ever suspected Greg of having a relationship with anyone?

Carrie: Yes, about three years ago I wondered about his relationship with his secretary, but when I asked him, Greg said there was nothing for me to worry about.

Note that the question "Have you ever had any relationship with anyone outside your marriage?" is purposefully vague. The intention is to inquire if there has ever been any relationship that has, at any time, replaced one spouse's affections for the other. The pastor, for example, should not exclude the possibility of a homosexual relationship being a disruptive factor in a marriage. And, of course, it is essential to the marriage counseling process for the pastor to know whether either spouse is engaged in a current extramarital relationship.

4. Most of the individual session will be devoted to the pastor's reviewing the areas of the questionnaire where more understanding seems needed. In the spirit of pastoral care, the pastor always asks questions in search of understanding, not for the intention of placing more blame on one spouse than on the other for their problems.

5. Before the session ends, the pastor should inquire if there has been sufficient opportunity to discuss whatever concerns the counselee wanted to review alone with the pastor. Then the pastor and the counselee should explore whether or not there is a need for a second individual session. At this stage the pastor should be willing to see both spouses individually for as many as, but no more than, two sessions each before seeing them together again.

6. In the individual counseling sessions, as in the joint sessions, the pastor will decide the best way to use faith and scripture resources as part of the counseling process. The use of scripture and prayer should emerge naturally from the interview to reflect the presence of God's love and to affirm the counselee's own best intentions and hopes, without ever becoming a manipulative exercise that denies the deeper conflicts in human emotions.

Reflecting on the data. In a spirit of prayerful deliberation, the pastor should consider all that has been learned in the individual sessions with each spouse. In that process, the pastor should also take account of what has been learned or observed about the husband and wife in these areas:

Mood. What is the person's prevailing mood? What are the dominant feelings? During a marital crisis, it is not unusual for spouses to experience considerable anger, anxiety, or depression. Disturbance in normal appetite and sleep patterns can be important clues as to how upset a person is over the marital tension. The pastor should also consider if there is any evidence of mood disturbance that is too pervasive to be wholly attributable to the marital crisis.

Judgment. An estimation should be made of each person's capacity for making appropriate decisions. How will this person respond in a crisis? Can this person make decisions that represent his or her own best interests?

Abstraction. Does the person think in highly abstract terms, or is the person more concrete about reaching decisions? For example, can the pastor talk with the husband about an egalitarian marriage in which role reversal from the traditional marriage is welcomed and valued? Or does the pastor have to speak in very specific language about the husband washing the dishes while his wife takes the car in to have the oil changed?

Reasoning and perception of reality. The pastor should note if there is any apparent irrational quality to a person's reasoning. Does the person's thinking follow a logical sequence that makes sense to the listener? Does either spouse reflect undue concern for what others may be thinking or saying about them? The pastor should take particular notice of any reports by a person that he or she has heard or seen objects or people that others would not have heard or seen if they had been present. Psychiatric assessment should be considered if the pastor observes or learns of any serious disturbance in a counselee's reasoning or perception of reality.

Faith resources. Is the person's faith a positive source of help during the marital crisis, or are the person's religious beliefs a source of disappointment or frustration? It is not extraordinary for faithful Christians to experience considerable doubt during a major crisis such as the deterioration of a marriage. The best pastoral care is to permit the person to express negative thoughts while offering pastoral support to the dimensions of faith that hold out a legitimate hope for the person in crisis.

It is appropriate for a pastor, following the individual counseling sessions with both spouses, to feel virtually overwhelmed with information and short on understanding. Indeed, a pastor should be suspicious about any firm conclusions that have emerged, because such conclusions may not fully take account of all of the complexities in the marriage conflict.

It is not the pastor's role, when meeting once again with the husband and wife together, to attempt to give them an elaborate explanation for why they are having marital problems. Some tentative ideas may be offered, but explanations that have the appearance of fixing the blame on one or the other spouse will jeopardize the counseling process. Rather, the pastor's sincere search for understanding will help the couple to take seriously their own search for understanding. The real question before the couple when they return together to see the pastor is not "What has the pastor figured out about our marriage?" but, rather, "What is it that each of us has been learning in this counseling process, and what are the best decisions each of us is willing to make now?"

Conclusion

The pastor has taken a significant step toward helping a troubled couple by scheduling individual sessions with each spouse and asking the husband and the wife to complete the Pastoral Marriage Counseling Questionnaire. The pastor's own search for understanding will help both spouses consider the broader context of their relationship tensions. In evaluating the information that comes from both spouses, the pastor will be guided by an attitude of concern for the marriage and by personal wisdom and experience about the complexity of being married. The pastor may also find it helpful to seek the consultation or recommendations of other professional persons. Specific ways the pastor can create a professional support system are discussed in chapter 5.

Though much may still be unclear about what the outcome of the counseling will be, the pastor continues the counseling process because, as Wayne Oates tells clergy, "You represent and symbolize far more than yourself."[8] So in the spirit of caring pastoral responsibility, and not because all the answers are apparent, the pastor can look forward now to meeting again with both marriage partners.

4

CONCLUDING
JOINT SESSIONS

When married couples are in trouble, they're going to fight it out more than quickly give up, find new partners, and join the singles scene. In the next decade, marriage and family counselors will be busier than divorce lawyers because of the difference that AIDS will make in our society.

—Pauline Boss[1]

"Hi, Ralph. Hi, Janet. I'm glad to see you. Come in and let's get started." Pastor Hanson is ready to see Ralph and Janet together about a week after their individual sessions with him. One of the decisions the pastor must make at this point is whether or not to interrupt the marriage counseling process.

Discontinuing the Marriage Counseling

The pastor may have gathered enough data to have decided that marriage counseling must be set aside in view of other equally, if not more, pressing concerns. Common issues that often make short-term marriage counseling questionable or impossible include current extramarital affairs, chemical addiction or abuse, physical or sexual abuse, or an emotional crisis requiring medical treatment. When any one of these issues must be discussed with the couple, and decisions are made about the pastor's continuing role as a counselor, *a primary rule should be that the pastor cannot function as both a counselor for the marriage and an ongoing counselor to one of the spouses.* The pastor can continue to be either a marriage counselor or a counselor to one spouse, but should not give any consideration to serving in both capacities or to being a counselor to both spouses individually, at the same time.

Extramarital affairs. While there are always exceptions to every rule, these guidelines should be considered by pastors when deciding how to handle extramarital affairs.

1. Marriage counseling has no possibility for being successful unless both spouses are committed to the marriage without other outside competing relationships. This guideline excludes the possibility of a spouse's continuing with marriage counseling in order to test whether to remain with the affair partner or the marriage partner.

2. If the person involved in the affair is not prepared to end that relationship, the pastor should recommend that the marriage counseling be discontinued. The explanation offered the other spouse, without disclosing the fact of the current affair, is that because of new information that has come to light in the individual session, the pastor is recommending personal counseling for the first spouse. So, if Ralph, during an individual session, has revealed that he is involved currently with another woman, the pastor would say to both Ralph and Janet that personal counseling for Ralph is recommended, with the marriage counseling being discontinued until Ralph has resolved some personal issues.

3. The pastor should also consider recommending supportive counseling for the other spouse, as well. Though the second spouse may or may not suspect that an affair is a factor in the marriage, individual supportive counseling can help the spouse cope with the considerable stress and uncertainty of having the marriage counseling discontinued.

Alcohol or chemical abuse. As most pastors know, the presence of alcohol or chemical abuse in a marriage creates a very difficult situation for the counselor. If, in fact, both spouses have, with some degree of willingness, come to the pastor for help, the pastor may regard that as a major victory in and of itself. Nonetheless, the pastoral counselor has several choices to consider.

1. The chemical abuse may be of such proportions that an addictive pattern is suspected. A significant test is if the marital conflicts and tension escalate every time one or both spouses use alcohol or other chemicals.

Until the addictive behavior is treated or discontinued, marriage counseling cannot be expected to be very helpful. The pastor needs to consider reporting this conclusion to both spouses, with the option that the spouse using chemicals go to a treatment center for evaluation and the other spouse become involved with Al-Anon. The pastor can indicate that, once those steps have been taken, counseling will be much more promising and the pastor will be very glad to work with the couple for the improvement of their marriage once the addictive use of chemicals has come to an end.

2. The pastor may determine that alcohol or chemical use is a factor in the marital conflicts, but it does not appear that an addictive pattern is present. Either spouse may acknowledge that on some occasions the use of alcohol has been excessive. However, the pastor must make a judgment, a decision that should be shared quite openly with both spouses. For example:

Pastor: Janet, in your individual session you talked about the times over the past two years, at office parties, when you know you have had too much to drink. Then you have come home, and you and Ralph invariably have gotten into an argument. This has happened three times in the past two years, the last time being about six months ago. Ralph, you said that you and Janet have talked about choosing some new friends who do not need to mix so much alcohol with their socializing. Neither one of you feels that the other has a pattern of regularly abusing alcohol. I am prepared to work with you on that assumption. I believe the test is whether in fact you can make genuine progress on your marriage, and whether the alcohol use stops being a factor in your marital conflicts.

Physical or sexual abuse. Marriage counseling will not be productive if either spouse feels intimidated by the other. The rebuilding of a marriage requires a context in which trust can be nurtured and there is encouragement to take risks and be vulnerable in sharing feelings. Renewed openness to one another will not take place if either spouse is living under the threat of physical or sexual retaliation.

The pastor should not continue the marriage counseling process if, in fact, the fear of physical or sexual abuse will prevent progress toward rebuilding trust and intimacy. The pastor's options include recommending treatment for the abuser either before resuming marriage counseling or concurrent with the marriage counseling. Other recommendations should include referring the victim of the abuse to a shelter or to his or her own individual counseling for the recovery of self-esteem and the consideration of the best choices for the victim, the marriage, and the family. A fuller discussion of pastoral options follows in chapter 5.

Referral for personal counseling. In the course of the individual sessions, it may become evident to the pastor that the emotional concerns of one of the spouses must be given as much consideration as the marriage problems. Of course, it may be difficult to discern whether a spouse's severe anxiety or depression is because of the marital tensions or a factor contributing to those tensions.

The pastor has the option of recommending that marriage counseling be discontinued until the spouse has completed treatment for the emotional concerns. The pastor may also suggest that the marriage counseling continue concurrently while the spouse is receiving individual therapy from another counselor. It is important, when making such a referral, that the pastor do so in such a manner as to minimize the appearance that the marriage problems are all attributable to the spouse being referred. Such a conclusion may all too readily be drawn by the other spouse, offering an excuse for not recognizing mutual responsibility for the problems in the marriage.

Proceeding with the Marriage Counseling

Pastor Hanson has decided there are no reasons for recommending to Ralph and Janet that the marriage counseling be discontinued. So the counseling session is opened with a question that asks both spouses to disclose any new ideas or feelings they have about their marriage and how to resolve their conflicts.

Pastor: I appreciate the effort both of you invested in responding to the questionnaire, and the concerns you discussed when I saw each of you separately. I am wondering now what learnings or feelings have occurred to each of you, either from the counseling process so far, or from any conversations you have had with each other, or just out of your own private thoughts.

Note that the pastor does not begin the session with any extended comments or analysis about what the pastor thinks is the problem or source of the marital conflict. Almost any analysis that the pastor offers at this point, even if it is requested by the husband and wife, will very likely be discounted or disregarded by one or both of them. Besides, what is really important is what the husband and wife think the problems are and any new ideas they have for resolving them together. Ralph and Janet might respond to the pastor's opening statement in this manner:

Ralph: I think I see more of a pattern now to our arguments than I recognized before we began this counseling. For example, we always have trouble talking about money, and that's been the case, now I think about it, ever since we've been married. I lost my job about six weeks after we were married, and Janet started paying the bills because she was afraid we would have to go to her parents for money. She had too much pride to do that, and we have been squabbling about money ever since. Then, after we fight about our finances, we start arguing about everything else. I think if we can get some kind of new understanding about money, half our struggles will be over.

Pastor: That sounds like an important insight. Have you shared this new thought with Janet?

Ralph: No, I haven't. There hasn't been enough time to sit down and talk. But I do think the money issue underlies a lot of our other problems and makes a lot of frustration for me.

Pastor: How do you see that, Janet? Would you just tell Ralph directly?

Janet: Sure. Ralph, you're certainly right about how nervous I have been about our disagreements over money. I remember as a kid how poor our family was, unable to pay the rent and living in fear of the whole family being put out on the street. I was embarrassed by how we had to live, and I vowed I would never see that happen to my own family. So maybe I get a little too uptight about finances. I'm ready to work with you toward resolving our disagreements about money, at least so we aren't fighting so much about it. I agree that if we stopped fighting about money, we wouldn't have nearly as much to be mad at each other about anymore. That would feel good!

This counseling session is off to a good start because (1) it builds on the spouses' own insights or learnings, (2) both spouses agree about the source of much of their conflict and are willing to work together on the problem, (3) they talk about themselves instead of blaming or attacking the other person, and (4) they are talking directly to each other instead of going through the pastor. These positive behaviors should be encouraged by the pastor at every opportunity, because they are the communication patterns necessary for restoring harmony to conflicted relationships.

Unfortunately, many marriage counseling sessions do not consist of such encouraging communication between the husband and wife. Unproductive and negative exchanges are readily recognized by the pastor when one spouse analyzes the other, makes unfavorable generalizations about the other, and frequently uses the word "you" in an accusatory manner. When attacking or blaming occurs, the pastor must take steps to interrupt that cycle by (1) *focusing on the blamer's feelings while drawing attention away from the spouse who is being blamed* and (2) *clarifying the blamer's issue(s)*. It is essential that the blamer feel that he or she has been heard and taken seriously, without the other spouse feeling attacked.

The success of the marriage counseling will often be determined by the pastoral counselor's skill in dealing with blaming by the two spouses. Pastor Hanson could have handled Ralph or Janet's blaming of each other in the following manner:

Ralph: Yes, it has become clearer to me in this process that Janet and I would not have so many fights if she weren't so uptight about money. And it's been going on ever since we've been married. She's like her mother. I don't mean to be disrespectful, but her mother does the same thing to her father. We aren't anywhere near bankruptcy, but she acts like we are. Half our arguments could easily be settled if she would adopt a more mature attitude about the realities of managing a family budget.

Janet: I agree that most of our arguments are about money, but my mother has nothing to do with it!

Ralph: You say that every time I raise the issue. You don't want to recognize that your anxieties about money simply get out of hand, and furthermore—

Pastor: Ralph, I want to interrupt here to see if I am understanding your concerns. I hear in your voice a sense of "fed-upness" around this issue, a good deal of impatience, hurt, and even anger or frustration. Is that right?

Ralph: Yes, you're right, Pastor. This is an old argument that has been going on since we were married, and my anger sometimes reaches the boiling point because of it, just as it did a moment ago.

Pastor: I think I might have heard you commenting on at least two or three issues through your anger, Ralph. First, making decisions about money is difficult for you and Janet.

Ralph: That's right.

Pastor: And when Janet is anxious about money, you, so to speak, get anxious about her anxiety.

Ralph: Well, something like that. When she's anxious she tells me what to do, and I don't need that.

Pastor: So a big issue for you is to avoid feeling that you are being controlled by Janet.

Ralph: I think that's at the heart of the matter.

At this point, the pastor has the option of engaging in further exploring and clarifying with Ralph, or of turning to Janet and asking for her views. The pastor's careful attention, while conversing directly with each spouse, to focusing on feelings and clarifying basic issues helps each spouse to learn, from a less threatening vantage point, important new information about the other's feelings and attitudes.

It is common for marriage counseling to include many exchanges of blaming and attacking between husband and wife. Sometimes the blaming is very obvious, and at other times it can be quite subtle. However, if the pastor listens to his or her own feeling reactions as well as to the words being said, there will usually be no mistaking when one spouse has attacked the other. Interrupting the attacking cycle is an essential task for the pastoral counselor, so productive communication can focus on the feelings and issues of each person. *Skill in helping couples is directly related to the pastor's ability to manage and refocus the attacking language that occurs in the marriage counseling sessions.*

Making changes. An important step in this second joint session is to explore with both partners what changes they think they are willing to make for the improvement of the marriage.

Pastor: When you came for marriage counseling it was probably much more clear to you what changes the other should make so there would be less conflict between you. However, I want to ask each of you what changes you yourself are prepared to make so there can be some lessening of the tension between you. I understand neither of you will make all the changes that the other wants, but the important thing is what you yourself want to do so things can be improved between the two of you.

Janet: You're right, there are things I won't be changing. For one thing, I am not going to change my concern about being sure we spend our money wisely and being certain that we save enough money for a rainy day. I frankly think, Ralph, that you want about the same things I want. What I will change is being more willing to spend time with you discussing our budget. Usually, I complain at the end of the month when the money has run out. Instead, I will be glad to talk with you at the beginning of the month, when both of us are in a better mood, so we can plan ahead. And then I will stop being so anxious and critical the rest of the time.

Ralph: I appreciate that, Janet. I know I won't be changing some of my basic ideas about handling money either. We'll have to learn somehow to compromise. I will change, however, by not making any more references to your mother. I know you don't like that, and it is not right. I will discuss only our issues, and I will be very glad to talk with you at the beginning of the month when our feelings are not quite so strong as they are at the end of the month.

Pastor Hanson can rightly feel that some significant progress has occurred with Janet and Ralph making these commitments to change. If couples are reluctant to talk about changes they each will make, or if they add sarcastic or disparaging comments such as "It won't do any good" or "I've already tried that and it didn't get us anywhere," the pastor's tentative assessment should be that resolution of the couple's conflicts will require longer-term counseling. Such an assessment should not necessarily be discouraging; rather, it should help the pastor set realistic expectations for what can or cannot be accomplished by the couple within the limits of short-term counseling.

Taking action. Under the best of circumstances, a troubled couple will be ready at this stage to commit themselves to engage in some "homework" together before the next—and final—joint counseling session. The pastor has used the second joint session to explore what changes each spouse is ready to make. Using their readiness to make some limited changes, the pastor's task now is to help the couple commit themselves to some specific tasks that will be new behavior for each of them for the sake of making positive changes in their relationship.

The pastor should exercise some caution and be wise about the assignment given to the couple. It is best if the partners decide for themselves what they will accomplish before the next counseling session. An assignment given or imposed on a couple by the pastor has considerably less likelihood of being attempted or accomplished. If husband and wife can design their own assignment, and thus have a greater sense of ownership for the project, they are more likely to complete the task. Pastor Hanson put the matter to Ralph and Janet in this fashion:

Pastor: Ralph and Janet, you both have shown your genuine interest in finding a better, less stressful routine for dealing with your finances. In order to change the unproductive patterns that have developed over the course of your marriage, some steps need to be taken in a new direction. I'm wondering what specific, concrete, new measures you both would be willing to take in the next week or so before we meet again.

Janet: I would like to propose that next Friday evening or next Sunday afternoon, for no more than half an hour, we review our financial commitments for the coming month.

Ralph: I want to sit down with you for that discussion, Janet, but Friday evening is the church softball game, and I always fall asleep after dinner on Sunday. Maybe we could do it *late* Sunday afternoon, about five o'clock. I like the idea of limiting our discussion to thirty minutes. Knowing that we have that limitation, I think we are more likely to have our conversation, since we know it won't go on forever.

Janet: OK, you have a date for Sunday at five o'clock in the afternoon.

This exchange illustrates the most promising manner in which a couple can undertake an assignment for homework between counseling sessions. It is important that the pastor help the couple design an assignment that is quite specific, in this case a half-hour discussion at a specific time on a specific day. Vague assignments such as "We'll be more understanding this week" or "We'll have more fun together this week," while having a good intention, will not be helpful. Vague assignments or commitments do not offer people specific behaviors they need to adopt in order to fulfill their good intentions. Furthermore, assignments or commitments to action should involve both spouses equally and be rather brief. If a commitment is unrealistically long, such as "listening to each other's feelings every day for an hour," it will defeat the couple almost from the outset. The assignment must be specific and easy to accomplish, so it is realistic to expect the couple to complete it successfully before the next counseling session. Whether or not they reduce their arguing very significantly, at least a couple can feel an important sense of accomplishment if they can report that in fact they did talk amicably with each other about money for half an hour on Sunday afternoon from five to five thirty.

When the counseling session does not go well. Pastors will have many marriage counseling sessions that do not follow the foregoing patterns. Conflicted couples have much difficulty communicating because so much pain has resulted from long-standing frustrated needs. Such couples create defensiveness in each other with little or no understanding for why each word they say widens the gulf between them. It is entirely possible that couples will come to the second joint session reporting they have learned nothing new, and furthermore they expect little or no positive change from their spouse. What does a pastor do in the presence of so much marital discord?

Above all, the pastor tries to communicate care and respect for both spouses, even though they are not feeling very caring or respectful of each other. Though a pastor may feel overwhelmed by the level of tension between the husband and wife, and may feel inept as a counselor, it is possible justifiably to take satisfaction in at least having arranged for the two spouses to be talking together under the best circumstances possible. Out of a sense of pastoral care for both persons, the pastor should not tolerate excessive arguing, and always has the right and responsibility to interrupt and intervene when the attacking and blaming detracts from the counseling process. Moreover, it is essential that the pastor resist being drawn by either spouse into taking sides. Indeed, the pastor may need to state clearly that the intention is not to take sides with either person but rather to try to listen and understand the concerns of both parties.

A pastor may find it easier to cope with tense marital counseling sessions by remembering that the primary goal of pastoral marriage counseling is to provide a context and a process in which both spouses

*can be heard and understood so both can then make their own best
decisions for their marriage, their family, and themselves.* Such a goal,
from a pastoral point of view, means that intense feelings must be
recognized and taken account of, and that one or both persons may
conclude that the marriage is no longer viable. If a pastor can do
marriage counseling from this viewpoint, there will be less anxiety
about counseling sessions that hold little or no promise for resolution
of deeply rooted and long-standing marital conflicts. Moreover, a pastor
can acknowledge all the pain and distrust that separate a couple and
still affirm both of them for their willingness at least to discuss their
problems in the presence of their pastor. The pastor may, in the midst
of a developing argument between two spouses, choose to express
some of the following thoughts:

Pastor: Ralph and Janet, I want to interrupt both of you, because I don't
feel the argument that is developing here will be helpful. It is
quite obvious to me that both of you feel very hurt by the many
misunderstandings that have developed between you over the
years. And tonight it may not seem to either of you that much
if any progress has been made. In fact, it has become so difficult
for each of you to trust the other that neither of you probably
could believe any promises for even the smallest changes the
other might make. You know it is my intention, as the pastor
of both of you, not to take sides. I care for each of you and for
your family. I am very concerned for the hurt each of you is
feeling. And I respect both of you for having the courage and
the strength to want to go through this counseling process.
Maybe we have done, now, all that can be done for this session.
I suggest we talk for a few minutes about what to expect in our
final session next week, and what might be done by both of you
before we meet again.

If the second joint session is filled with much conflict and tension, a
pastor will be quite successful just to acknowledge to both spouses the
full strength of the feelings that are being expressed, clarify the issues
that concern each person, and do so in such a way that both spouses
talk mainly about themselves and as little as possible about the other
person. Even if no progress is made toward the resolution of their
conflicts, at least husband and wife will have been given the opportunity
to hear and understand each other perhaps a little better than they
have in the past.

Ending the second joint session. Before the session with both
spouses comes to a close, the pastor should remind them that the next

session is the last session they had all agreed to, and that one of the purposes of the final session is to assess all that has been accomplished and not accomplished in the counseling process. In most instances, the pastor should allow an interval of at least a week or more between the second joint session and the final one. Time permits persons to adopt a more conciliatory perspective, if the differences are not too great. On the other hand, if the problems continue to be severe or overwhelming at this point, it is important that the couple meet with the pastor within a week's time or sooner in order to consider what the next course of action should be.

After helping the couple to anticipate the next joint session, the pastor may choose to close with a prayer that recognizes and affirms the stress both spouses are feeling, acknowledges the presence and guidance of God's love, and asks for God's care to be with both spouses and their family as important decisions are being made.

Preparation for the Final Counseling Session

Before the earlier individual sessions with each spouse, the pastor read the questionnaires from both persons and determined the principal issues to be explored during the counseling sessions. The pastor should also prepare for the final counseling session, by thinking through and briefly writing down responses to these questions:

1. What are the presenting problems that husband and wife have said need to be resolved?

2. From the pastor's viewpoint, what related issues must be taken into account with the original problems named by the spouses? What is the severity of those related issues?

3. What, in the pastor's judgment, has been accomplished so far in the counseling process toward the resolution of the couple's problems?

4. What are the necessary and appropriate actions that still need to be taken for all the main problems and issues in the marriage to be resolved satisfactorily for both husband and wife?

By giving preliminary thought to these questions, and by answering them as specifically as possible, the pastor will be in a better position to offer the best help to the couple when they return for the third joint counseling session.

Pastor Hanson made the following notes to the four questions in preparation for the meeting with Ralph and Janet.

1. Janet is upset because Ralph has become too involved in his job over the past two years. Success has gone to his head, so it seems he has forgotten about her and the children. Ralph feels Janet is too

controlling and wants to run his life. He is tired of listening to her complaining and, frankly, is reluctant to be home more often because all he hears when he is home is Janet's fault-finding. Both Ralph and Janet agree that they also have a problem when they discuss and try to reach agreement on budget and money issues.

2. There are two other related issues. Ralph's self-esteem is not very solid. He does not seem very sure of himself and appears to be overly influenced by his boss at work. This is a serious problem if Ralph is to adopt a more realistic attitude toward his job. Janet's parents live only a mile and a half from Janet and Ralph. They have never been very fond of Ralph, and Janet gets a sympathetic ear from her mother when she's upset about him. The marriage would certainly be helped if Janet had other sources of support besides her parents.

3. So far, the counseling sessions have been moderately productive. Ralph and Janet both want their marriage to survive this current crisis period. They have agreed to find a better way to discuss their financial problems. And Ralph acknowledges he should spend more time at home with Janet and the family. Both Ralph and Janet have responded well to the counseling sessions and have found some better ways to talk with each other than their former pattern of blaming each other.

4. Remaining steps for Ralph and Janet's problems to be resolved:

Janet should seek other female friends for support besides her parents (and especially her mother).

Ralph should consider personal counseling with another counselor so he can work on his own self-esteem issues, particularly as they relate to his work.

Both Ralph and Janet should continue with at least four more marriage counseling sessions, but on a less frequent basis, for support of their new communication patterns.

Engaging in this process of preparation for the third joint session clarifies the pastor's own observations and thinking up to this point. More information may emerge during the final counseling session that will influence the pastor's conclusions. The views of husband and wife are equally important. But by going through a process of organized and systematic reflection before the final session, the pastor will be better prepared to help Ralph and Janet assess the progress they have made and the steps they need to take for greater harmony in their marriage.

The Process in the Final Counseling Session

The pastor not only should have reached tentative conclusions about the couple's progress but should also have decided, before the session begins, how the final session will be structured. It is not acceptable for a pastor to have no idea at all, before the last session begins, about what should happen for the final counseling session to be productive. The pastor should consider the following plan for that session:

1. The pastor begins by inquiring how the husband and wife are presently relating to each other. It is important for the pastor to know at the opening of the final session on what kind of terms the two spouses are now dealing with each other.

2. Next, the pastor points out the purpose of the final session: that the main focus will be assessing what has been accomplished and what the couple still needs to do for their marriage.

3. Before beginning the assessment, the pastor should ask the couple what they did about their assignment from the previous session.

4. The pastor and the couple make a careful assessment of the progress achieved as well as what has failed to be accomplished so far through the counseling.

5. The pastor and the couple reach conclusions together about the three options: ending all counseling with this final session, referring one or both of the spouses to another counseling source, or recontracting with the pastor for further counseling either for both as a couple or for one of them individually.

There should be no surprise to the couple about this outline for the final counseling session, because it reflects the original plan discussed and agreed to at the very first session. The outline, however, should be considered flexible. Although each point should somehow be included in the process of the session, varying amounts of time, as needed, may be spent at any point in the process. Sometimes, more time will be given to the assessment phase, and on other occasions more time will be needed for dealing with the assignment from the previous session or for discussing the pastor's recommendation of a referral to another counselor. The following excerpts of counseling dialogue show how a pastor may follow the structured outline for the session.

1. Checking out present feelings. It is important, at the outset, for the pastor to make a point of asking the partners how things are: that is, how are they feeling toward each other as the session begins. Some couples are quite expert at covering up fights with each other, so no one recognizes they are at war in spite of their laughter. It is not unusual for a counseling session to be near conclusion, the pastor assuming that all has gone well, and then to find out the couple had a fight in the car on the way over and are considering separation, with the husband moving out that night. While being very important, this initial step in the last session should take only a few minutes.

2. Defining the purpose of the session. After inquiring briefly about the present status of the relationship, the pastor states what is to be accomplished in the counseling session.

Pastor: Ralph and Janet, when you began this marriage counseling process several weeks ago, we agreed that the purpose of this particular session would be mainly for assessment and evaluation of what has been accomplished for your marriage and what still remains to be done. And then, in the light of that assessment, we can consider what the best courses of action should be for the possibility of any further counseling. So after I hear how you handled the assignment you promised to work on during the past week, I suggest we move right to the assessment. Does that agree with your understanding of the purpose for tonight?

If the pastor fails to state the purpose of the session right at the outset, the direction can easily be lost or go astray. Particularly if there is a high level of tension or disagreement between the spouses, the focus of the session can readily be diverted to the issues of conflict, and the element of assessment be lost in the process. The pastor may wish to ask if either partner wants to put any other items on the agenda in addition to the assessment process.

Pastor: Besides considering what has been accomplished and what still needs to be achieved for your marriage, are there any other concerns that either of you wants to deal with this evening?

Janet: Yes, I'm afraid that Ralph and I may lose all the progress we made when I tell him that I invited my parents for supper tomorrow night, and I didn't get a chance to talk to him before inviting them. I'm really concerned, and I think it would be better for Ralph and me to talk about it here with you.

Pastor: We could talk about it for a few minutes before we do the assessing. But I don't want to take too much time away from the assessing process.

Janet: That's fine. I'll just feel better once we get the matter cleared up.

The purpose of the final session is now fully understood by the pastor and the couple. Janet's issue can be dealt with before the assessment process without jeopardizing the main task focus for the session.

3. Reviewing the assignment. The success of the couple in completing their assignment can be another gauge for the pastor's evaluation of their growth. However, care must be taken about drawing any firm conclusions from what the couple reports. In many instances, couples will say that they did not have much success with the assignment, no matter how realistic and concrete the assigned task may have been. Pastors can expect that couples with severe conflicts will hardly ever attempt the assignment, much less complete it, and even couples who are making good progress may or may not handle their assignments successfully. In those instances when the assignment has been completed by the couple, it will usually be viewed by them as a significant step toward growth in their relationship.

The pastor may choose to ask the couple questions about the assignment.

> "Were there any learnings or discoveries for you as you worked together?"
>
> "What was the hardest part for you?"
>
> "What did you enjoy the most?"
>
> "Were some of the problems you encountered in doing the assignment typical in any respect of the problems you have had in other areas of your marriage?"
>
> "What is the next assignment you both would like to design for the improvement of your marriage?"

4. Assessing progress through counseling. The pastor may initiate this phase of the session with a statement like this:

Pastor: Now, Janet and Ralph, we have come to the central purpose for this session as we evaluate what has been achieved and what still remains to be accomplished so you both can feel much better about your marriage. I expect there will be some agreement, but also that you both may see things a bit differently. Let's begin with each of you saying what you feel has definitely been accomplished over the past weeks of counseling.

The process of evaluation can offer the couple a good opportunity for understanding better the sources of conflict in the marriage. Because the focus of the evaluation is necessarily upon the past four or more weeks instead of the past four or fourteen years, observations can be more specific, and each spouse can easily recall events referred to by the other. It is easier to discuss an argument that is only two weeks old than a conflict that began more than two years ago.

By the same token, the couple's principal conflicts over the years will more than likely be evident in the interactions of the preceding weeks. A couple that has difficulty finding quality time for communication will have to have dealt somehow with that issue after beginning the marriage counseling. Or a couple that generally disagrees on how to handle money will most likely have had at least some occasions in the past month for facing that issue. Assessment of their relationship since beginning counseling will help most couples examine their main sources of trouble.

A pastor does well to be a bit skeptical about reports from spouses that extraordinary progress has occurred in dealing with their problems. As a rule, marriages do not get into trouble overnight, and rarely do enormous changes for the better occur instantaneously. Of course, it is very gratifying if a couple declares that all problems have been resolved in the space of four or five weeks of counseling. However, it is more realistic for a pastor to keep in mind that real growth in even the best of marriages is a slow process. That is not to say that four weeks of counseling cannot make an enormous difference in changing the course of a marriage, but hard work will still be required of both spouses if the changes for the better are to be continued.

A realistic and honest approach is the best attitude for both the pastor and the couple to evaluate any changes that have occurred in the marital relationship.

Janet: I think that Ralph and I have talked more in the past four weeks than in the previous four years. I have felt less tension being around Ralph. We aren't fighting nearly as much, and we have even been able to talk about some of our financial problems.

Ralph: I haven't felt so criticized by Janet, and it has been better in the evenings after work. I've really looked forward to coming home over the past month. It's true that we have had some fruitful conversations about our financial problems, but we still have a lot of money problems to resolve. We don't agree about our credit cards, for example. We just got a statement with what Janet considers an outrageous balance due on it.

Pastor: I'm glad to hear that you both can point to some significant areas of progress. Maybe you have turned the corner with regard to some of your problems and are seeing some promising changes for the better. It is clear, too, that there are important areas of your relationship that you still need to work on together for improvement.

The pastor, having made a private assessment before the counseling session, should wait before sharing this evaluation until both spouses have expressed their own ideas. Both husband and wife are less likely to resist the pastor's recommendations if they have first fully participated in the evaluation process. The pastor may even encourage the couple to be more specific about what further work needs to be done for the marriage.

Pastor: I am wondering now exactly what you both feel needs more attention so your marriage can be more nearly what both of you want.

Ralph: It's pretty clear to me that I need to find ways to leave my job behind at the office and spend more meaningful time communicating with my family. I get too wrapped up in my work; it is on my mind all the time. That's still a real problem for me. I also think Janet and I need to keep working on finding better ways to make decisions about our money.

Janet: I agree with you, Ralph. I want to communicate more with you, and I need to stop being so picky and complaining. We haven't said too much about it, but I think my parents are a problem for us. If I were to find other friends, I wouldn't have to be so dependent on my mother, and that would be better for both of us.

Now the pastor can share his or her own observations. The pastor's evaluation helps a couple to focus their efforts toward marital growth.

Pastor: I have reached conclusions similar to what both of you have said. You both have demonstrated a genuine commitment to improving your marriage and are beginning to rediscover more satisfying ways for intimate communication and problem-solving. There is a lot more work to be done in that area. Yes, Janet, your parents are important to you, but friendships for you with other women would benefit both you and Ralph. And Ralph, it has seemed to me that much of your self-esteem is identified with your job, a pattern that has developed for quite a long time. Breaking that pattern could bring much improvement in your home relationships, but working with a counselor by yourself on that issue might be the most productive approach for you at this time.

In the assessment process it certainly is appropriate for the pastor to invite comments from the couple regarding the structured marriage counseling process itself, which has just been completed. The pastor can learn from parishioners' comments about what has been helpful or not helpful in the process. However, neither the pastor nor the couple should dwell on criticizing the counseling process instead of evaluating what has or has not been accomplished for the marriage. Nor should a pastor permit a couple to blame the pastor's supposed inexperience or ineptness as a counselor for the marriage's getting worse instead of better. Presumably parishioners have freely chosen to participate in the process, which was thoroughly outlined and discussed at the initial counseling session. Moreover, the pastor should never claim to be an expert marriage counselor but rather a pastor doing what is appropriate for a pastor to do in offering care to troubled individuals and couples. In most instances, excessive criticism of the pastor or the counseling process should be viewed by the pastor as an effort by the critics to avoid examination of themselves and their marriage. Adopting this perspective may help a pastor to feel less defensive when a counselee is obviously shifting the focus away from the marriage to the pastor or the procedures that have been followed. If valid and legitimate criticisms are offered regarding the pastor's counseling skills, the pastor may benefit by discussing these comments with another pastor or professional person.

5. Making recommendations for continued marriage growth. If their marital problems were in the early stages, many couples will find much benefit through the short-term marriage counseling process. Sometimes a couple will be ready to end the marriage counseling with this final session, and both the couple and the pastor will feel good that their problems are under control. Other couples will end the counseling without a strong sense of accomplishment, but somehow determined to survive and tolerate their problems for the next twenty years as they have for the past twenty years.

If further counseling with the pastor is desired by the couple, the pastor must make some important personal decisions. Many pastors have rightly decided that the priorities for their pastoral time do not permit extended involvement in pastoral counseling. Moreover, many pastors will also conclude that their expertise in counseling does not qualify them to proceed beyond an initial four to six counseling sessions. Other pastors will decide that they can see a couple on a less frequent basis another three to five times.

In some instances it can be quite difficult for a pastor to make the decision to refer a couple or an individual to another professional resource. In fact, the couple may have a good relationship with the pastor, and thus further progress may be jeopardized if a referral is made to another counselor. The pastor must evaluate the need to feel important, to feel that "this couple won't make it if I, as their pastor, abandon them now." Whereas such a conclusion may be rooted in some reality, it also may be grounded in a pastor's inflated need to nurture parishioners' dependence. *A pastor who is not in a specialized counseling ministry and who chooses to go beyond ten to twelve formal counseling sessions with a couple should examine carefully the rationale and personal motivations for such extended involvement.* That is not to say that longer-term pastoral counseling is always inappropriate, but in the context of the varied demands and responsibilities of the parish ministry, such commitments to pastoral counseling should be carefully evaluated. *Often, a good referral to another counselor can be the best expression of responsible pastoral care.*

Generally, two elements are necessary for a good referral. The first is the pastor's respected professional judgment that a referral is in order. It is unlikely, in most cases, that a pastor's recommendation of a referral will come as a surprise. A person may have known for many months, for example, that anxiety and continued difficulty sleeping and concentrating should have medical attention. But the pastor's professional judgment will often be necessary to provide the motivation for the parishioner to take the steps that have been avoided much too long.

The second essential element in a good referral is the pastor's recommendation of a resource with which the pastor has a personal acquaintance, so the referral can be made with genuine enthusiasm. If a pastor says to a distraught parishioner, "I recommend that you see a psychiatrist for your depression," in most instances the parishioner will not follow through on the referral. But if a pastor can say, "I recommend that you see Dr. Brown at the Medical Center; I know Dr. Brown and have referred others to her and have felt good about her care for those people," the parishioner is much more likely to act on the recommendation.

It should be noted that it is equally important for a pastor not to overrate the person to whom the parishioner is being referred. To say, "Dr. Brown has helped everyone I have ever sent, and I am sure that she is exactly the person for you so you will never be depressed again," is to do a disservice to both the parishioner and to Dr. Brown. A parishioner whose expectations have been misled often will not continue with the new professional person because the "miracle cure" does not happen as the parishioner had been led by the pastor to believe it would. Obviously, for a pastor to be able to make effective referrals, it is necessary to make every effort to become well acquainted with the varied professional resources in the community.

When a referral is made to another professional person, in most instances it is better for parishioners to make their own appointments. By observing that practice, the parishioner is allowed to take responsibility for his or her own well-being, and the pastor avoids the professional embarrassment of a parishioner's failing to show up for an appointment the pastor has made.[2]

When working with a couple and making a referral, it is important for the pastor to keep in mind *the principle of balance,* so neither spouse is put in the position of appearing to be the main source of the marital conflict. When reflecting upon Ralph and Janet's marriage, Pastor Hanson had concluded that it would be appropriate to refer Ralph to another counselor so he could develop his self-esteem apart from his excessive involvement and identification with his work. The risk for the pastor in referring Ralph to a psychologist or psychiatrist is that Janet will conclude that the pastor is confirming her suspicions that there is "something wrong" with Ralph, and that whatever is "wrong" is causing the marriage problems. Whenever possible, the pastor wants to avoid creating a situation in which one spouse can use the pastor's recommendations for blaming all marital problems on the other spouse. Unless there is shared responsibility for a marriage, and for the conflicts in the relationship, there is little possibility for those conflicts to be happily and constructively resolved. Even in extreme situations where one spouse is unquestionably abusing alcohol or is being physically abusive, for which a necessary referral to specialized treatment is warranted, the marriage will require the mutual investment and work of both spouses during and after the specialized treatment for the one spouse.

Insofar as possible, when making recommendations in the final joint session, the pastor should make suggestions and referrals that equally involve both spouses. Thus, Pastor Hanson might have said the following to Janet and Ralph.

Pastor: I have a recommendation that I want to offer to both of you, and then a recommendation to each of you separately. First, I believe that you have made a good start toward improving your communication, especially around the budget and money problems you have had for so long. If you want to continue your work with me, I suggest that we schedule four more sessions, two to three weeks apart, with the focus on improving communication for decisions about money. As your communication improves in that area, it may very well improve in other areas too.

Second, I have a recommendation for each of you. Ralph, you have acknowledged how much your self-esteem has been tied up for you with your work, so I want to refer you to a psychologist I am acquainted with, Dr. Weber, who I believe could help you make progress toward gaining a better perspective about yourself and the meaning your work has for you. Janet, I feel it is equally important for you to extend your personal support network beyond your parents and children. It is good for you to be involved with your parents; nonetheless, the cultivation of three to five new friendships could greatly benefit not only you but also how you and Ralph relate to each other. In other words, the plan is to help Ralph become more involved at home

with Janet and to help Janet to involve herself more outside
the home so all her needs are not focused on Ralph and her
family. How do these recommendations sound to you?

The pastor has made specific recommendations that include individual, balanced suggestions for both spouses and concludes by asking
for Ralph's and Janet's reactions. If either spouse is surprised by the
recommendations or resistant to the pastor's suggestions, a discussion
of those reservations may result in the decision that the recommendations are, after all, worthy of being acted upon by both partners.

Continuing pastoral care. The process of short-term pastoral marriage counseling takes place within the larger context of general pastoral care. As parishioners, the partners remain within the pastoral
oversight and responsibility of the pastor, even if one or both spouses
are referred to another professional mental health resource.

In the best of circumstances, a pastor will have resources in the
community to whom parishioners can be referred, and a working relationship—with the counselee's permission—can be continued between the other professional and the pastor. Unfortunately, in some
communities there is an atmosphere of distrust, and in some cases
disrespect, between the clergy and other mental health professionals.
Such suspicion does not work best for the parishioner who needs to
seek the help of a psychologist or psychiatrist. When a parishioner has
been referred to another counselor, the pastor's proper role is to continue normal pastoral contact and care but not to establish or maintain
an ongoing counseling relationship with the person.

Continuing pastoral care, in the cases where a couple ends the marriage counseling process, should include a follow-up pastoral visit in
the couple's home within two months. Such an occasion should be
arranged ahead of time over the telephone. The purpose of the visit
should not be for serious marriage counseling, but rather to indicate
the pastor's sincere interest in how things are going. If it should become
apparent in the course of the visit that there are further marital issues
to be worked on, the pastor should consider scheduling an appointment
at the church office within the next week instead of renewing counseling
in the couple's living room when the original purpose had been only
to have a pastoral visit.

Finally, the pastor may choose to end the brief marriage counseling
process by reasserting the intention to be a pastor equally to both
spouses.

Pastor: Janet and Ralph, I have appreciated the opportunity to work
with you during this critical time of challenge and growth in
your relationship. I care very much about both of you and your

family, as I hope you know. I have tried to avoid taking sides, and that is also my intent for the future. If either of you feels a need, again, to come to me with concerns about your marriage, I recommend that both of you become involved together in further counseling. If, for some reason, it seems advisable for me to be a counseling resource for one of you individually, then I probably will not be able to be your marriage counselor again. We will need to talk about that if the occasion should arise. I want to be an impartial pastor to both of you. I believe that is how I can best help you.

Conclusion

The purpose of the brief marriage counseling model is to chart a course for both pastor and parishioners for intervention in conflicted marriages. When both the pastor and the partners have agreed to follow the process that has been outlined, they then have a procedure for gathering essential information, discussing the main sources of conflict, and committing to new courses of action toward resolution. Moreover, the process leads to a definite ending point for assessment and recommendations so the couple can take all the necessary steps for finding resolution of long-standing problems. Throughout the process, the pastor's role is not that of expert marriage counselor, though in many instances pastors are quite skilled in their counseling methods. Rather, the pastor's primary role and authority are defined by the pastoral office, rooted in the pastoral care tradition of the church. Utilizing the brief marriage counseling model within the context of their office and authority, many pastors will help countless couples find reconciliation who otherwise would find no help at all.

5

SPECIAL CONCERNS
IN MARRIAGE COUNSELING

I will go so far as to say that never can a man completely understand a woman, nor a woman a man.

—**Paul Tournier**[1]

The short-term model for pastoral marriage counseling is a valuable resource for parish pastors in much of their work with couples in crisis. However, in many situations, a pastor will be faced with the decision of whether to use the model, as it has been outlined, or adapt or modify the basic plan. Moreover, every pastor will be confronted with numerous questions when dealing with the unique and varied demands brought by individual couples for pastoral care and counseling. The purpose of this chapter is to discuss major themes and issues for guiding the pastor's intervention with couples and families undergoing a marital crisis.

Professional Support and Training

Both a major strength and a weakness of professional parish ministry is the fact that most clergy function rather well, in many situations, as isolated practitioners. The personalities of most persons drawn to the ordained ministry are such that they rather easily lead others in times of crisis and feel confident about their own resources for problem-solving. Consequently, it is the nature of most parish clergy not to seek consultative help or support as they make serious pastoral judgments affecting the lives of their parishioners.

By contrast, most mental health professionals are very careful about maintaining regular opportunities for professional review of their counseling cases and of their relationships with counselees. Involvement in other people's intense, emotional crises will always evoke feelings in both the pastor and the counselee toward each other. Experienced pastors know that discussions of sexual material can stir a sexual response within both counselee and counselor. The occurrence of a wide range of such feelings in the pastor and parishioner is very natural and cannot be avoided. However, if the behaviors prompted by those feelings, especially the pastor's behaviors, are not properly reviewed and managed, the counseling process can be unhelpful or even damaging for the parishioner. Miller and Jackson have stated the issue succinctly:

> These reactions are particularly dangerous when they happen to fit into a pattern of transference from the client, as when a dependent client finds a therapist with rescue needs, or a seductive client finds a counselor with a strong need to be admired and loved. Every counselor sets out with the fantasy that "It could never happen to me," but many become ensnared in these difficult situations. Where a pastoral role is involved, such relationships can further evolve into emotional or even financial blackmail and the potential loss of parish and profession.[2]

Counseling both partners of a marriage does not lessen the possibility for the pastor's own feelings to become a hindrance to the couple's best interests. Indeed, the pastoral involvement with two persons in a single counseling relationship can increase the possibility for the pastor's viewpoint and behavior to become distracted and distorted. *It is a wise pastor who intentionally creates a viable support system with other professional persons for reviewing pastoral counseling cases and for knowing the best resources in the community for referral.* Having a network of professionals with whom to consult regularly is the best way for a pastor to ensure providing effective pastoral care and counseling to troubled couples. It is not sufficient for a pastor just to read a book or books about the skills necessary for pastoral counseling. Ongoing supervision and consultation, and advanced clinical training when possible, are necessary for skills to be enhanced and serious counseling errors to be avoided. Any pastor who engages in marriage counseling beyond the short-term model should take every step to have a sound network for counseling supervision and consultation.

In many parish settings it will take only a little imaginative thinking for a pastor to make use of other professional persons. Many physicians or psychologists will welcome an inquiry from a pastor who would like to "brown bag" once a month and, over lunch, review counseling concerns. Usually a pastor can make such an informal arrangement at no cost or fee. Another option, of course, is for a pastor to covenant with a group of other pastors to meet regularly to discuss counseling cases. Always there is the risk of exposing oneself professionally to other professional colleagues, but what can be learned for the benefit of the parishioners one is trying to help makes the risk worthwhile.

An important question is whether interprofessional consultation violates the confidentiality of parishioners. A pastor is always correct to be concerned that the details of people's lives shared in one's office or study remain confidential. With that concern in mind, a pastor has two options when seeking consultation from other professional persons. One possibility is for a pastor to tell counselees about the pastor's wish to discuss their situation with another professional person and to secure their written permission to do this. Another choice is simply to disguise names and identifying data and discuss only the essential case dynamics, without informing the counselee that any outside consultation is taking place. Whatever steps the pastor takes, the parishioner's rights to confidentiality must be protected. However, it is a responsible act on the part of the pastor to seek professional consultation so that the parishioner receives the best help possible.

Increasingly, more clinical training opportunities are available to pastors through church-related agencies and pastoral counseling centers. Pastors should be aware of the American Association of Pastoral Counselors (AAPC), which encourages the continued training of clergy in the disciplines of pastoral counseling. The AAPC has several levels of affiliation and membership and has set standards for the clinical training of pastors in the basic skills of counseling. Pastors should seek out the professional persons in their area who are associated with the AAPC and also participate in training programs that meet AAPC standards. Further information about the AAPC and resources in one's area may be obtained through the national office of the AAPC at 9508A Lee Highway, Fairfax, Virginia 22031.

An additional important resource is the American Association for Marriage and Family Therapy (AAMFT). The AAMFT sets clinical standards for membership that include marriage and family therapists in many disciplines, including social workers and psychologists. By writing to the national office of the AAMFT, a pastor can locate AAMFT members in the area who could be contacted for possible referrals or as consultants for the pastor. The address of the AAMFT is 1717 K Street NW, #407, Washington, D.C. 20006.

Avoiding a Sexist Bias

The experienced pastor monitors carefully her or his own feelings in the counseling interaction with the parishioner. But more pervasive than immediate feeling responses are the pastor's personal, cultural, and theological biases. Although aware of strong feeling reactions to a parishioner, a pastor may be quite unaware of personal attitudinal biases that can have an even greater effect upon the counseling relationship. One of the most unfortunate biases a pastor can have is the unexamined assumption that one understands the opposite sex and knows the proper role members of the opposite sex should take in society, and particularly in marriage relationships.

In the final pages of her book *In a Different Voice,* Carol Gilligan makes this observation:

> My research suggests that men and women may speak different languages that they assume are the same, using similar words to encode disparate experiences of self and social relationships. Because these languages share an overlapping moral vocabulary, they contain a propensity for systematic mistranslation, creating misunderstandings which impede communication and limit the potential for cooperation and care in relationships.[3]

The pastoral counselor, whether female or male, should never forget how profoundly different are the disparate experiences of men and women. Younger counselors may readily and wholeheartedly endorse and follow such a recommendation. But in many instances it is the older, more experienced counselors who need to exercise the greater caution—precisely because of their experience in years of life and counseling—about their assumptions regarding the inner world and needs of persons of the opposite gender. Indeed, anytime a counselor hears a person of the opposite sex recounting their personal concerns and problems, it is wise to adopt the attitude of listening carefully as if hearing the words for the first time. While some of our understandings of both men and women may often be generally accurate, we must never forget that we are always a foreigner eavesdropping on another culture when we try to understand the concerns of persons of the opposite sex. Thus it will be with the utmost respect, and with a sense of awe, that the pastoral counselor goes about the task and challenge of trying to understand the personal experiences of both a husband and a wife.

For these reasons, the pastoral counselor should never lose sight of the obvious fact that in marriage counseling there are always two persons of one sex in the counseling room and only one person of the opposite sex. In many if not most counseling situations, the sexual imbalance in the room will not be a strong negative factor for the spouse in the minority. But the pastor should never assume that the imbalance is not an issue, however subtly. Most certainly the sexual imbalance is a block to effective counseling when the pastor takes the side of the spouse of the same sex. Male clergy are especially suscep-tible to contributing to such an imbalance if they hold the view that the wife is supposed to do her husband's bidding. *It is the pastor's responsibility and task to view both spouses as human beings equally loved by God and therefore of equal worth and dignity.* Because most of us as males and females are greatly influenced by cultural patterns and values that do not respect the essential worth of every person, as pastoral counselors we must be especially careful to respect the essential dignity of both spouses.[4]

Basic Themes in Marriage Counseling

Whether or not the pastoral counselor adheres to the short-term model described in this book or chooses to do longer-term counseling with couples, variations on certain themes will recur. Recognition of these themes, in whatever words parishioners use to describe them, will help the pastor to focus on basic issues in the conflicted marriage.

David Luecke has described four essential relationship systems that are major areas needing work by troubled couples. Luecke says that conflicted marriages usually reveal breakdowns somewhere in regard to the systems of compatibility, cooperation, intimacy, and emotional support.[5]

Compatibility issues focus on differences in values and life-style preferences. She may love rock music, and he wants to listen to classical music. Or he always wants to take her to his family's annual reunion, but she prefers to spend vacations at the shore, as far away from family as possible. One of them believes money is for spending, and the other feels that money is for saving for a rainy day. All married persons bring their own unique patterns of personal values and preferences to their marriage, and inevitably one person's preferences and tastes will clash with those of the partner. Every married couple must somehow find ways to deal with basic differences and creatively overcome the challenges to a workable level of compatibility in their relationship.

Cooperation is necessary for a couple to achieve satisfactory compatibility. Many couples, unfortunately, are not able to find ways to cooperate, and consequently when they negotiate one or both go away feeling like losers. When cooperation has been achieved, both partners feel like winners. Problems in communication and failure to work together in the spirit of a united partnership will usually make it very difficult for a couple to reach a satisfying level of cooperation.

Intimacy needs in marriage have spiritual, sexual, conversational, companionship, emotional, and problem-solving dimensions. Charlotte H. and Howard J. Clinebell have also identified these additional major opportunities for intimacy: intellectual, aesthetic, creative, recreational, work, crisis and commitment.[6] Intimacy cannot occur unless there is self-disclosure and risk-taking. And satisfactory intimacy ordinarily does not happen unless there is close interaction between the spouses in most dimensions of their marriage. Husbands often feel that sex is the surest route to satisfactory intimacy. Wives often resist the quick equating of sex with intimacy and insist first upon relational intimacy in other areas of the marriage. Both partners are correct; the fullest experience of intimacy will come when closeness is experienced and risked at every level of the marriage.

Emotional support means "we can lean on each other in the midst of our personal storms." At some time, all persons need to feel taken care of, nurtured, and reassured that their partner is on their side. Often emotional support can best be shown by couples learning more effective listening and communication skills. To be thoroughly and carefully heard can leave one with much assurance of being supported. Physically being held or caressed can be very nurturing for either spouse when facing a period of troubling anxiety, turmoil, or depression. Marriage without emotional support is very lonely. The pastor will often hear troubled husbands and wives struggling to reach out in new ways in order to find the mutual caring and support they need so much from each other.

Two other basic themes the pastor will recognize in most marriages are perceived equity and a balanced distribution of power. Reciprocally equitable behavior in marriage has been identified by William Lederer and Don Jackson as a pattern of quid pro quo essential to all stable marriage relationships. This pattern is based on perceived equity that is satisfying to both the wife and the husband.

> The *quid pro quo* process is an unconscious effort of both partners to assure themselves that they are equals, that they are peers. It is a technique enabling each to preserve . . . dignity and self-esteem. Their equality may not be apparent to the world at large; it may be based upon values meaningless to anyone else, yet serve to maintain the relationship because the people involved perceive their behavioral balance as fair and mutually satisfying.[7]

Human beings do not like to be in relationships that feel unjust, especially in a marriage. Many of the complaints a pastor hears are a variation on the theme that one spouse does not feel certain aspects of the marriage are fair. "How come he gets to watch football all Sunday afternoon while I iron his shirts for the coming week?" "It's not fair that I work hard all day at the office too, and when I come home I have to cook the meals and run the washer and do the cleaning. He lives here too! Why can't he at least clean the toilet?" "I keep the cars running and take care of everything outside the house. What has she got to complain about?"

Sometimes the pastor can be quite direct about addressing the issue of fairness and perceived equity.

Pastor: Both of you are upset because in some important areas you do not feel things are fair, and so your marriage is suffering. I'd like to help you find some workable arrangements so you both can feel your marriage relationship is a fair one.

Most couples will welcome such a statement from their pastor. In some instances the pastor will need to emphasize the importance for equity to be equally perceived by both spouses. Though he may think it is up to her to clean the toilet, as long as she does not feel it is fair, full equity will be missing. Until both spouses are persuaded that their marriage is a truly fair relationship, distressing tension will continue.

The other theme of balanced power relates to the capacity of both spouses for influencing or changing the rules of the marriage to the benefit of personal needs or preferences. The pastor will often see conflicted marriages in which both persons feel they have much less power than their partner for negotiating how they are to relate with each other. It is not unusual for both spouses in the same marriage to feel they have less power than their partner. Both persons will often report that the other is the one who wins most of the conflicts and arguments!

The process of marriage counseling, with a third person present to monitor the negotiating process, usually ensures that both spouses will exercise similar degrees of influence toward the restructuring of their marriage. The pastor can often help the recovery of a better balance of power by pointing out the behaviors of either spouse that manipulate or take unfair advantage of the other person.

Pastor: Tim, I have noticed that each time Pam begins to outline new ways for the two of you to handle money, you interrupt her in order to present your own viewpoint. Pam's ideas will not be given full consideration if she is not permitted the opportunity to present them as fully as you present yours. You recall Pam said earlier that she feels intimidated by the way you put down her ideas? Interrupting Pam can only reinforce this sense of intimidation.

With most couples the pastor will often be dealing with issues related to perceived fairness and equal power for renegotiation of the basic rules of the marriage. The ability to recognize these two basic themes as well as the common themes of compatibility, cooperation, intimacy, and emotional support will greatly enhance the pastor's effectiveness for helping most troubled couples.

Pastoral Counseling for Sexual Problems

Married couples can engage in no more complex activity than their attempts to have a successful sexual union. Sexual feelings and responses relate deeply with every other feeling that one may have about oneself. Needs for being nurtured, pleasured, and satisfied are invariably involved in sexual interaction with one's partner. Moreover, the need to feel one is a caring spouse and a satisfying lover is very important for both husband and wife. David Mace has summarized just how complex human sexual union can be. As he points out, both spouses must have normal and healthy sex organs. Each must have a heterosexual drive to be attracted to a person of the opposite sex. Both husband and wife must find each other sexually attractive, and both need to be relatively free from negative or blocking feelings such as guilt or resentment. Additionally, Mace observes that the couple

> must manage successfully each individual act of intercourse so that it is satisfying to both. They must agree about how frequently, and when and where, they will come together sexually. They must keep a proper balance between their sex desires and their personal relationship with one another. And they must control procreation, by some means of contraception, in a way that is acceptable to both. Complications can arise in any or all of these areas.[8]

Sex therapist Helen Singer Kaplan has outlined other potential areas for problems that can make it difficult for couples to achieve a happy sexual adjustment in their marriage. In some instances husbands and wives are naive about the basic physiological needs of their own bodies and the bodies of their partner. Some women never experience sexual satisfaction because they are unaware of the stimulation their bodies require, and their husbands assume they should achieve sexual arousal as rapidly as they do. Unconscious resistance to the pleasure of sex may prompt some persons to avoid intimacy that can lead to sexual arousal. Anxiety associated with sex can be experienced as a fear of failure and concern for adequate performance, which can quickly lead to a man losing his erection. Some persons block their own sexual enjoyment by taking the role of a spectator or judge at their own lovemaking. Others may simply not allow themselves to feel the intensity of their own erotic emotions and responses to their partner. Kaplan also points out that poor or inadequate communication between spouses can perpetuate sexual problems that a couple might ordinarily resolve if there was open, trusting communication.[9]

Anxiety over the AIDS (Acquired Immune Deficiency Syndrome) virus is becoming an increasing concern for even monogamous, heterosexual couples. AIDS has taught many people that when they have sex with someone, they are in fact having sex with everyone else their partner has sexually encountered, with respect to exposure to AIDS. Therefore, it is becoming a common procedure for a man and a woman anticipating their initial sexual encounter first to disclose to each other the names or backgrounds of all their former sex partners. Couples who have a trusting and faithful relationship may never be troubled about concerns that one or the other is or has become a carrier of the AIDS virus.

Where such trust is not present in a marriage, the threat of possible exposure to AIDS may become a source of significant anxiety, inhibiting sexual response and enjoyment between husband and wife.

As the pastor deals with couples having any of the sexual problems outlined below, attention should be given to any accompanying concerns regarding AIDS that seem associated with the particular area of sexual conflict. Also, in some instances pastors will find themselves confronted with the ethical dilemma of whether unsuspecting spouses should be told of their partners' extramarital sexual liaisons because of the possible exposure to AIDS for both husband and wife.

The husband's sexual problems. The pastor may hear concerns from either spouse about the following difficulties for the husband.

1. *Impotence,* or the failure of the husband to maintain an erection for a sufficient amount of time for the satisfactory completion of sexual intercourse. The word "impotence" is an unfortunate use of language because it carries negative overtones. On the other hand, the term conveys much of the psychological meaning for men when they lose their capacity to maintain an erection: that is, they often feel they have lost an important source of their power, their personal effectiveness as a male. While erectile failure can be disturbing for the husband, it can also be troubling for the wife who wants to be understanding but also feels frustrated by repeated unsuccessful attempts at sexual intercourse.

Primary impotence, or the failure ever to have had a satisfactory erection for intercourse, is a more serious condition. Secondary impotence, which is far more common, occurs after a previous history of successful erectile experiences. Secondary impotence is said to have occurred when the husband is having erectile failure at least 25 percent of the time that intercourse is attempted. Professional sex therapists report that about half the male population has experienced occasional or brief periods of erectile failure, sometimes due to fatigue, depression, or pressing emotional concerns. Failure to achieve a satisfactory erection can occur in men of all ages and from any socioeconomic group.

Pastors should realize that the abuse of alcohol or other drugs can inhibit the physiological processes necessary for a male erection. Hormone imbalance can be a factor, as well as physical causes such as neurological diseases, diabetes, and arteriosclerosis. Of course, psychological factors in the marital relationship can play a major role in erectile failure, such as unresolved conflict or the husband's fear of failing to perform adequately. Ironically, the erectile response to sexual stimulation cannot be willed by a male, which often leads to increased frustration. Trying harder, therefore, is not the solution to this marital problem. Rather, improvement often occurs when the husband ceases to be preoccupied with the problem and recovers once again his spontaneous enjoyment and response to sexual play and stimulation from his wife.

2. *Premature ejaculation* refers to a man's inability to control his orgasm, resulting in orgasm during sexual intercourse before his partner reaches her own climax. Clinicians have not agreed on a precise definition of this condition. Some researchers have based their definition on the specific amount of time a man can refrain from ejaculation. Others use the term to describe a more chronic situation in which the male ejaculates more than 50 percent of the time before his wife reaches orgasm.

Regardless of the difficulty in reaching a precise definition, a quick or uncontrollable ejaculatory response is a common occurrence. Marital tension arises when the husband's early orgasm leads to disappointment and frustration of his wife's efforts to achieve her own sexual satisfaction. Some males are insensitive and unconcerned about their wife's disappointment. Other husbands are quite concerned that they cannot control their sexual response sufficiently in order to be a satisfying sex partner. A husband's early or uncontrolled orgasmic response can occur in any marriage and is not necessarily reflective of marital conflicts.

Therapists often use treatment techniques that increase the husband's attentiveness to his own erotic arousal. The wife may be trained in using a "squeeze" technique on her husband's erect penis which helps to delay his ejaculatory response.

3. Some couples may report the husband's *inability to ejaculate* while his penis is in his wife's vagina. There can be a wide diversity in the extent of this problem, from the man who has never experienced orgasm to the husband who may occasionally not be able to reach a climax. Husbands and wives may explain that he can be successfully stimulated manually or orally, but once insertion in his wife's vagina has occurred, attempts to reach an orgasm are often unsuccessful.

Although it might be assumed that some wives might be glad to have a sex partner who does not reach a premature or quick climax, her husband's recurring failure to have an orgasm can be very frustrating for a wife. Sexual intercourse in marriage includes the exchange of mutual pleasuring, and it is disappointing for partners to feel they have not pleasured their spouse as they themselves have been satisfied.

An occasional inhibition of the male ejaculatory response may be due to frequent intercourse or brief periods of fatigue or anxiety. Other causes include diabetes, illnesses involving the nervous system, the use of some drugs, hormone imbalance, and psychological conflicts between husband and wife. Sex therapists often use techniques that involve the wife manually stimulating her husband nearly to the point of uncontrolled ejaculation before his penis is inserted in her vagina.

4. The husband's *low sex drive* may be a concern for the couple. Although men are thought to be preoccupied with sexual interests and fantasies, and although many wives are distracted by their husband's frequent overtures for sexual activity, it can be troubling to both spouses when the husband feels and demonstrates little or no sexual interest in his wife. The pastor does well to inquire in an individual session with the husband if he has another sex partner. However, if the husband denies any extramarital sexual activity, the counselor should advise the couple to consider a physical examination for the husband while also exploring marital issues and the husband's possible excessive preoccupation with business, career, or other outside interests.

The wife's sexual problems. Either spouse may discuss with the pastor the following areas of sexual concern for the wife.

1. The wife may have *little or no desire for or pleasure from sexual activity* and intercourse with her husband. All too often the word "frigid" has been used, ordinarily by frustrated husbands, to describe a woman's apparent disinterest in sexual play and intercourse. This is an imprecise and pejorative term and should not be used by the pastor.

It is not unusual to hear a husband or a wife report that her sexual appetite requires less sexual activity than her husband's level of interest. Because of this difference in needs, it is easy for one spouse to conclude or imply that the other is "abnormal," "frigid," or "oversexed." A few women in fact have never experienced erotic feelings or desired sexual activity. It is more common for some women to have enjoyed sexual experiences and orgasm but to go through phases in their marriage when their felt need for sexual satisfaction is minimal. Often the difference in sexual needs and interests between spouses can create extreme marital tension. Many women feel they must "do their duty" to satisfy their husbands, and some men simply seek extramarital sexual release when their sexual needs are not met by their wives.

The pastor should be careful about reaching premature conclusions about the causes for a wife's apparent lack of interest in sexual activity with her husband. Just because she may usually want sexual intercourse less often than her husband does not mean a wife is abnormal. Obviously, the emotional climate of the marriage can greatly affect a woman's response to her husband. Moreover, the sensitivity and attentiveness of a considerate husband is a primary factor in a wife's response to sexual intimacy. Current use of drugs, illness, hormone balance, and early sexual history can be significant factors that influence the interest a woman has for erotic stimulation. Counselors and sex therapists will want to understand as much as possible about a woman, both present and past, before reaching a conclusion about why she may not be responding to her husband. In most instances, it will be essential for the couple, especially the husband, to realize that the wife's lack of interest in sexual activity is a joint problem for them to work on with sensitivity and caring for each other, and not just *her* problem!

2. The *wife may not be having orgasms* after a previous history of orgasmic experience, or she may never have experienced an orgasm. Failure to have an orgasm can occur in women who otherwise experience sexual arousal and want to have sexual intimacy with their husbands. Despite their need for a sexual climax, they are unable to achieve an orgasm or do so only with great difficulty. Many women are unable to achieve orgasm during coitus except through simultaneous manual stimulation of their clitoris.

Psychological factors can be a strong influence in a woman's sexual response and her inability to relax and experience an orgasm. As a rule, the husband's efforts to be his wife's therapist in attempts to explain why she is inhibited will not be helpful. Work with a female counselor is probably the best way for inorgasmic women to explore the psychological conflicts that inhibit their response. Physiological factors also must be explored, such as illness, use of drugs, or hormone imbalance.

Treatment by a sex therapist will have the goal of helping the woman to focus on her own erotic responses, including learning to achieve and enjoy orgasm through masturbation. It is essential that a husband be sensitive to his wife's need for adequate love play and preparation for coitus. As with other sexual concerns, it is important that husband and wife view the wife's failure to achieve orgasm to her satisfaction as *their* problem and not just hers.

3. *Vaginismus* is a condition occurring in some women because of the involuntary spasm of the muscles at the vaginal entrance. When the woman anticipates penetration during sexual intercourse or a pelvic examination in the doctor's office, the closing of the entrance to the vagina makes the introduction of any object virtually impossible without pain and discomfort to the woman. Often, women with this condition are fearful of sexual intercourse, though they may be sexually responsive and enjoy sexual play as long as it does not lead to intercourse. Frequently, such women have been the victims of some traumatic sexual experience in the past, or they have been reared in a religiously repressive environment that placed negative values on sexual expression. Women reporting vaginismus may be in either troubled or otherwise untroubled marriages. However, because vaginismus makes satisfactory sexual intercourse virtually impossible, the marital

relationship will be under increased strain until treatment and relief are found for the condition.

Vaginismus can only be diagnosed with certainty through a pelvic examination. Sex therapists use techniques involving the husband with his wife as she goes through procedures to reverse the involuntary spasm of the vaginal muscles. The condition is highly responsive to treatment. Ordinarily, counseling is also necessary in order to help the woman resolve any associated emotional traumas.

Either husband or wife may also report experiencing pain associated with the act of sexual intercourse. The woman may describe aching, irritation, or burning in the vagina, as well as severe pain during penile thrusting. Men may have discomfort related to intercourse, the painful symptoms occurring in the several organs associated with male sexual functioning. This painful consequence of sexual intercourse in both men and woman is called "dyspareunia."

The pastor's response. Most clergy are not specialists in sex counseling, nor is it necessary for in-depth counseling to be initiated in areas for which the pastor has no particular training or background. However, pastors can be helpful to couples with sexual concerns if certain guidelines and principles are followed.

1. Recognize that the discussion of sexual material can be sexually stimulating for the counselor as well as the parishioner. Awareness of this fact can help the pastor to exercise personal judgment about exploring sexual matters. However, to the extent the pastor feels comfortable dealing with sexual issues, the pastor's sensitive and nonjudgmental caring can help unblock confusion and guilt associated for many people around sexual concerns.[10]

2. Referral to a medical doctor is always appropriate when dealing with sexual problems. A thorough medical examination is generally necessary before a sexual problem can be properly diagnosed and treated.

3. The pastor can fill an important educative role by offering correct sexual information to either husband or wife. Clearly, the pastor has a moral and professional responsibility to be certain that the information is correct and not reflecting a particular bias. As an educator, the pastor can liberate some couples from sexual myths, such as the myth of the simultaneous climax being a measure of successful coitus. (For a more detailed discussion of human sexual problems, the pastor is referred to Helen Singer Kaplan, *The New Sex Therapy;* Masters and Johnson, *Human Sexual Inadequacy;* Masters, Johnson, and Kolodny, *Masters and Johnson on Sex and Human Loving;* and F. Philip Rice, *Sexual Problems in Marriage.* These books are listed at the back of the book under Recommended Reading.)

4. A pastor may also be helpful to parishioners by explaining to them that masturbation, in and of itself, is physiologically a natural act. Couples may be helped with the information that masturbation in fact can have an appropriate function in a marriage when understood and accepted by both partners as a natural means for relieving sexual tension when one's partner is not available.

5. David Mace has aptly described "The Uses of Noncoital Sex."[11] Many couples can be helped to discover wider expressions of their sexual love by experimenting with physical pleasuring without the expectation or demand of intercourse. Activities that lead to orgasm without intercourse can add a joyful and freeing new dimension to marital lovemaking.

6. Encourage both partners to learn to be respectful and appreciative of each other's sexual needs, preferences, and limitations. Each person is a unique sexual being. Respect for and accommodation to one's partner's sexual distinctiveness is a requirement for satisfactory marital adjustment. A couple is more likely to create an environment for meeting each other's needs when both feel a clear sense of respect and appreciation from their partner.

7. Generally, sexual adjustment in marriage is more positive when both partners take responsibility for telling their spouse what they need. Operating on the assumption that one's partner will automatically know what one needs can lead to much misunderstanding and frustration in the sexual relationship.

8. Make referrals to persons who are qualified specialists in counseling for sexual problems. Ordinarily, a married couple should be referred together to a sex therapist. If a person wants to deal individually with sexual concerns, that person should generally be referred to a therapist of the same gender.

Responding to Marital Violence

Counseling pastors can no longer remain naive or uninformed about the wide prevalence of domestic violence in our society. Data on marital violence have led researchers to dismaying conclusions.

> It is estimated that in one out of two marriages at least one incident of violence, probably more, will occur. In one out of five marriages the violence will be ongoing, with five or more incidents per year. At the extreme, episodes will happen monthly, weekly, or even more frequently.[12]

After surveying statistics on the number of women beaten by their husbands, Rita-Lou Clarke concluded that one of four husbands are violent to their wives at some time in the marriage.[13]

Unfortunately, the church and the clergy in too many instances have reinforced social patterns that lead to domestic and marital violence.

The following observations should be a matter of concern to all pastoral counselors.

> Researchers . . . have identified religious institutions as perpetrators of wife beating because of their patriarchal attitudes. While not all denominations are patriarchal, Christian women from patriarchal churches have religious beliefs which hinder them from stopping the cycle of violence in their marital relationships.
>
> In addition to the strong influence of their religious values, Christian battered women may be hindered by an unsympathetic clergy. A minister who equates authority with control within his church may also support the right of the husband to control his wife. . . . One study . . . found that, compared to friends, relatives, lawyers, police, women's groups, and psychologists, clergy had the lowest success rate and the highest negative influence in counseling battered women.[14]

Although husbands can be the victims of marital violence, most often wives are the ones who suffer from physical and sexual abuse. The abuser will frequently be heard to argue that "I have my rights, too. She shouldn't nag at me and holler all the time. She knows I can't take it when she starts screaming at me!" The underlying assumption, which may also be appealing to many pastors, is that the victim has purposely or unwittingly made the abuser strike out. In other words, "She asked for it."

In many instances clergy have focused their counseling attention on the wife when she is the victim, and the results of the counseling have not been positive for her. Frequently, it takes a great deal of courage for a woman finally to come to her pastor to disclose the abuse that has been happening at home. In many situations, the husband does not come with his wife and is unwilling to come to subsequent counseling sessions. Many clergy, in the past, have counseled the abused woman to return home and, in the spirit of prayer, become more accommodating to her husband's needs so he will not have reason or cause to attack her again. The assumption is that if the woman is sufficiently compliant to her husband's demands, marital harmony will be restored. Another counseling approach has been to direct the woman to examine her personality to see what is wrong with her that any man would find her hard to live with and be driven to acts of violence because of the defects in her character. Certainly, the assumption goes, if she were less hostile or less passive or less seductive or whatever, there would be no reason for her husband to beat her up. This has been called "blaming the victim."

Marital violence is destructive to marriages and families for three reasons. First, violence can result in injury, often very serious injury. No relationship is healthy if one partner is suffering physical injury in the midst of conflict with the other. Second, just the threat or possibility of physical injury invariably intimidates the victim. Once physical abuse has occurred and the boundary against violence has been crossed, the victim lives with the constant fear that physical injury can happen again. Intimidation unbalances the power for negotiation in the marriage and leaves the victim in a subordinate and often powerless position. A growing and mutually satisfying marriage is not possible where intimidation has left one of the partners in a vulnerable and victimized position. Third, children are placed in an emotionally unsettling and unstable environment when they see or sense that physical violence is occurring between their parents. Not only may the children fear for their own safety, they most certainly know that the reality of such violence in the home threatens the stability and existence of their parents' marriage and the future of the family as a unit.

Domestic violence requires pastoral intervention that may be quite different from what a minister is used to offering. Probing, insight-oriented counseling with either spouse ordinarily will not interrupt an established pattern of marital violence. Direct intervention is necessary, and the pastor must take a clear stand against any continuing abuse. The following guidelines can help a counselor plan an effective pastoral strategy for intervention in marital violence.

1. *Always take seriously any suggestion of marital violence.* The pastor should explore very carefully any reference by either spouse to physical intimidation or abuse. Make clear that such abuse is a very serious matter. Inquire when, how often, and under what circumstances such abuse has taken place. Be careful of dismissing a violent event because "it only happened one time three years ago." Also, out of fairness to both spouses, the pastor should assess exactly what has happened in order not to attribute to one spouse more abusive behavior than has actually occurred. However, it must always be remembered that if one spouse feels at all intimidated by the other, for whatever reason, such intimidation most likely plays a major disruptive role in the marital relationship.

2. *Assess the victim's position.* The victim feels powerless and in many respects is in a position with few options. The counselor needs to take a realistic view of all available choices. For example, a pastor might say to a woman that the pastor wants to talk with her husband about his abusive behavior. However, the wife may feel that such a conversation with her husband can only make things worse, and she would prefer to find reasons to leave home for a day or two when she senses her husband's mood becoming tense. Although a pastor might wish to deal directly with the husband and his threatening behavior, the wife's wishes and concerns must be the final guide. The pastor should not make any intervention that the victim does not know of and approve. The victim, powerless in the marriage, must be permitted to have the power of knowledge and consent in the counseling process.

3. *The pastoral counselor takes a verbal stand.* In most counseling situations, the pastor will remain neutral and not express any judgment about a counselee's behavior. However, in the case of marital violence, it is essential that the pastor say clearly that there is no place for any physical abuse or violence in a marriage, except of course in the case of self-defense against physical attack. While affirming that the behaviors or words of either spouse can be severely damaging both psychologically and emotionally, the pastor should state clearly that no amount of emotional abuse justifies a physical attack. Moreover, the pastor should add that both spouses are responsible for their own behavior, regardless of what the other person may say or do. The abusing spouse needs to be confronted with the fact that nothing the other person does, no matter how outrageous, can justify an abusive response.

4. *Review with the victim all options for help.* The victim should clearly understand every resource that is available for help. The pastor should be able to give to the victim telephone numbers for locating shelters if it becomes necessary to leave home. The victim should also be advised of resources in the community for the treatment of abusers and specialized counseling for the victims of domestic abuse. Moreover, the pastor should review with the victim plans of action that might include the enlisting of help from neighbors, friends, or relatives. It is essential that the victim not continue to feel powerless. Knowing all one's options and having several plans for action can give a victim greater confidence for handling the next crisis.

5. *Refer the abuser for specialized treatment.* If a treatment program is available within the area, the pastor should refer the abusing spouse to that program. In most cases of domestic violence, and particularly those in which a pattern of abuse can be recognized, neither promises by the abuser nor counseling by the pastor will interrupt the abusive behavior. The pastor can explain to the abuser that any treatment program will make an initial evaluation in order to determine if the abuser has a problem that can in fact be treated by that particular program. Some persons are more willing to accept a referral from the pastor when they understand they are going first for an evaluation and not immediately into a treatment program.

6. *Continuing marriage counseling.* If the abusing spouse does enter a treatment program, the pastor should plan to continue the marriage counseling process in consultation with the abuser's counselor in the treatment program.

7. ***The abuser is not accepted for treatment.*** It is possible that many pastors will not have nearby resources to which an abusing spouse can be referred. Or in some instances a treatment program may reject a referred spouse because there is not a clear enough history of abuse for the abuser to be accepted into the program. Thus, the pastor is left as the primary counselor for a marriage in which threatening intimidation is a major factor. Once again, it is the pastor's responsibility to declare that progress in the marriage cannot occur and that marriage counseling will be to no avail if there is any continued abuse. Moreover, the pastor should tell both spouses of the pastor's intention to support and encourage the victim to follow through with appropriate measures in order to avoid any personal injury or harm and any possible injury to the children, should any abusive threats or crises occur in the future. *While the pastor should be neutral in expressing pastoral care toward both spouses, the pastor cannot remain neutral about encouraging both spouses to take the necessary steps to bring the marital violence to an end.*

When Divorce Is the Choice

Marriage and family therapists know very well the reason for so much of the pain experienced by persons who must go through the legal dissolution of their marriage.

> The craziest thing about marriages is that one cannot get divorced. We just do not seem to make it out of intimate relationships. It is obviously possible to divide up the property and to decide not to live together any more, but it is impossible to go back to being single. Marriage is like a stew that has irreversible and irrevocable characteristics that the parts cannot be rid of. Divorce is leaving part of the self behind, like the rabbit who escapes the trap by gnawing one leg off.[15]

Hardly anyone who has gone through a divorce will describe it as having been the easy way out. Instead, most persons find divorce to be the last way out of an intolerably painful relationship that has lost all potential for reconciliation and growth. And as pointed out above so clearly, divorce is a painful leaving behind of a part of one's self as much as it is a way out for the sake of one's sanity. Even when a divorce promises relief from indescribable relationship conflicts, there is always the loss of leaving behind that part of one's self which for a while was at one with the life of the former partner.

Experienced pastors know that marriage counseling can very well result in the choice by one or both spouses to take steps for separation and eventual divorce. Though many divorcing couples understandably find it very difficult to talk to one another without bitterness and accusations, when possible the pastor should offer to work with such couples in divorce counseling. The following invitation can be offered:

Pastor: I know that both of you have very reluctantly come to the conclusion that a divorce is now the only option before you. In spite of the deep hurt each of you feels in your own way, and in spite of the mixed feelings you have about each other, I would like to continue working with both of you together. I make that invitation for three reasons.

First, by continuing in a form of divorce counseling, there may be sufficient resolution to the pain each of you is feeling so that you can at least part with a sense of genuine respect for each other.

Second, you will continue to be in communication with each other around the concerns of the children. Counseling together now may help you to communicate better about the children, and that will of course be of great benefit to them.

Third, lawyers are often essential in a divorce, but any communicating you can manage to do directly with each other about the details can save a lot of involvement and indirect communication between the two of you through your lawyers.

The purpose of divorce counseling is not to reestablish the marriage. Although a pastor would be thrilled if a broken marital relationship could be restored, it is important that the pastor and both spouses be clear that divorce counseling is for the purpose of bringing as much reconciliation as possible in preparation for a divorce. If the pastor can be an agent for the reduction of pain, misunderstanding, bitterness, and hatred, then in most instances much will have been accomplished. And a pastor may especially feel a sense of accomplishment if the divorcing couple invites the pastor, or accepts the pastor's offer to officiate at a brief service, before God and a few witnesses, recognizing the dissolution of the marriage. Such a service can be a rich symbol for a couple that God's grace and healing are just as much with them at their parting as when they became husband and wife.[16]

Clergy should also be aware of mediation counseling resources when they exist in the community. Mediation counselors specialize in helping divorcing couples work out legal details and arrangements for a divorce in a professional environment that controls hostility and encourages communication apart from the involvement of lawyers.

The Children of Conflicted Marriages

A recent survey has shown that over half of all children of elementary school age interviewed said they feel afraid when their parents have arguments.[17] Children of any age sense the levels of tension occurring between their parents. Children may not hear all the words nor understand all the issues, but they certainly can feel very deeply the emotional and disruptive impact of long-standing alienation between their parents.

The counseling pastor cannot ignore the children who are the emotional victims of their parents' fighting. Andrew Lester has rightly declared that pastors have a critical responsibility for making sensitive interventions in the lives of troubled children.

> We know that many of the emotional, relational, and spiritual problems with which adults suffer result from childhood crises that were not resolved creatively. Effective pastoral care with a child in crisis may prevent the crisis from having a lifelong debilitating effect on the child's emotional, physical, and spiritual health.[18]

Some parents will ask whether children are affected by marital conflict or divorce. The answer is always yes. Frequently, what the parents are wondering is if their children will necessarily have serious behavioral problems or in other ways appear not to be "adjusting" to the disruption of the family. Whether or not children have obvious adjustment problems, all children are affected by continuing conflict between their parents. The question is not whether children are affected by parental strife, but to what *degree* they are affected. Indeed, many children cope with the emotional strain of family tensions by being model students in school and church. Through outstanding academic or athletic achievement, young people can create a substitute environment of support and affirmation in place of what is threatened and unavailable to them in a family upset by continuing parental conflict. Obviously, reports of children having trouble at school, or indications through a child's behavior problems at church, can be clear tipoffs that a child most likely is not coping effectively with the marital problems at home. However, in every instance where a couple with children is having serious marital problems, the pastor will always be correct in assuming that the children are personally faced with a serious crisis.

In his book *Pastoral Care with Children in Crisis,* Andrew Lester describes in detail numerous approaches for pastoral care and counseling to be offered to children.[19] Underlying Lester's recommendations is, first, the importance for pastors to take notice of the needs of their young parishioners. Second, the pastor should in some tangible ways demonstrate to the children that their pastor knows who they are, genuinely cares about them, and has the time to talk with them. It is best, of course, when a pastor has laid the groundwork in church before a child begins to experience disruption in the family. When a pastoral relationship has already been established, it is more natural for the child to recognize that the pastor is a sincerely caring friend who can be a source of support and understanding.

Although only a few pastors may wish to develop a specialized counseling ministry with children, any pastor who is a friend to young parishioners can have a positive pastoral influence upon young lives. To children, the pastor represents God and the church. Just the fact that such a representative has remembered a child's name and spoken for a few minutes can help the child feel that God is a friend to be trusted when relationships at home are frightening. The caring pastor who offers counseling to couples with children will always be trying to find sensitive and creative ways to show children that their pastor has a genuine interest in them and their concerns.

Conclusion: The Challenge and the Call

Instituted by God, marriage holds out to men and women the possibility for the greatest joy and the worst emotional pain. Marriage certainly is, as David and Vera Mace have described it, a relationship of "terrifying closeness."[20] And, obviously, the children of the generations that follow every marriage are profoundly influenced by the marital conflicts and decisions of their parents, their grandparents, and even their great-grandparents. Because so much is at stake in modern marriages, the purpose of this book has been to enable pastors to respond and intervene, in a professionally responsible manner, in the troubled marriages of their parishioners.

The challenge to the church in its heritage and tradition of the pastoral care of souls is to be present wherever alienation disrupts human lives and relationships. Marriage counseling is a responsibility and a call that must be taken seriously by every pastor and can hardly be avoided by any pastor. It is hoped that the short-term marriage counseling model will help many pastors to discover more opportunities to bring care and counseling to troubled couples. May the results be an increasing number of marriages where love, stability, and growth have been restored because a pastor took steps to be an effective instrument in the exciting process of God's healing for broken relationships.

Pastoral Marriage
Counseling Questionnaire*

The purpose of this questionnaire is to help you reflect on issues and dynamics related to your marriage. This information will also assist your pastor to explore with you the various resources and options you and your partner have for resolving conflicts and strengthening your relationship. Though it takes time to complete these questions, many persons find doing so helps them to clarify their feelings and understandings as they put their thoughts on paper.

Do not share your written responses with your partner. After your counseling sessions with your pastor, this questionnaire will be returned to you.

Name _____ Age _____

Occupation _____

Current address _____

Home phone number _____ Work phone number _____

---

* Pastors are granted permission and are encouraged to use this questionnaire with their parishioners. Additional space for writing should be added when the questionnaire is reproduced.

Spouse's name _____ Age _____

Spouse's occupation _____

Spouse's current address _____.

Spouse's home phone _____ Spouse's work phone _____

Courtship and Marriage

1. How did you and your spouse first meet?

2. What were your reasons for marrying your spouse?

3. What was your honeymoon like, and what were your feelings about it?

4. Do you have any children? If yes, give their names, ages, and school grades.

5. Where do children outside the home live?

6. If any children are no longer living, when and how did they die?

7. Have you or your spouse been married before? If so, when and how did that marriage end?

8. Do the current problems in your marriage include any of the following? Circle those that apply.

a. Lack of communication
b. Sexual or physical abuse
c. Infidelity
d. In-law involvement
e. Finances
f. Problems relating to children

g. Work-related problems
h. Alcohol or chemical abuse
i. Sexual adjustment problems
j. Unfulfilled emotional needs
k. Lack of spiritual growth
l. Other (specify)

On a blank sheet, please elaborate on each of the items you circled.

9. For your marriage to be more satisfying, what do you think your spouse needs to change?

10. For your marriage to be more satisfying, what do you think you need to change within or about yourself?

11. What are you willing to change?

Family of Origin

12. Father's name _____

Age if living _____ Deceased?: Date _____ Age _____

Occupation _____

13. Mother's name _____

Age if living _____ Deceased?: Date _____ Age _____

Occupation _____

14. Do you have any brothers or sisters, living or dead? If so, list their names and ages, beginning with the oldest. Place yourself in the list.

15. Describe your relationship with your father until you left home.

16. Describe your relationship with your mother until you left home.

17. In a few sentences state how your family of origin was unique or different from other families.

18. Upon reflection, what do you think your role was in your family of origin? That is, what did you make possible for your family by your presence and your behavior?

19. Is there any history of alcohol or chemical abuse in your present or original family? If yes, please describe.

20. Is there any history of sexual or physical abuse in your present or original family? If yes, please describe.

Personal Information

21. Do you take any medication? If yes, please give name and dosage.

    Prescribed by _____ When _____

    For what condition? _____

    Any side effects? _____

22. Have you ever had any serious illness or hospitalization? If yes, please describe and give dates.

23. How much regular coffee, tea, cola, or other caffeine-containing beverages do you drink?

24. What is your current appetite and eating pattern?

25. Describe any gain or loss in your weight.

26. Describe your sleep pattern: when you sleep and any difficulties you associate with sleeping.

27. Is your religion or faith a positive or a negative resource for you and for your marriage? Please explain.

28. Please describe any work-related concerns or conflicts you are currently experiencing.

29. Have you ever had any previous professional counseling help? If yes, give dates, the purpose of the counseling, and the name of the counselor or agency.

30. Have you or your spouse ever tried to commit suicide? If yes, give the date(s) and briefly describe the circumstances.

31. Describe yourself as you understand your personality.

32. Please describe briefly, and give the dates, for the times in your life when you have had any thoughts, feelings, or experiences that were unusual or disturbing for you.

NOTES

Chapter 1: Introduction to Pastoral Marriage Counseling

1. Randall Collins, *Sociology of Marriage and the Family: Gender, Love, and Property* (Chicago: Nelson-Hall, Publishers, 1985), p. 262.

2. "Annual Summary of Births, Marriages, Divorces, and Deaths: United States, 1986," National Center for Health Statistics, *Monthly Vital Statistics Report,* vol. 35, no. 13 (August 1987), pp. 3–4.

3. Gibson Winter, *Love and Conflict* (Garden City, N.Y.: Doubleday & Co., 1958), p. 183.

4. Paul W. Pruyser, *The Minister as Diagnostician: Personal Problems in Pastoral Perspective* (Philadelphia: Westminster Press, 1976), p. 25.

5. Thomas C. Oden, *Pastoral Theology: Essentials of Ministry* (San Francisco: Harper & Row, 1983), p. 179.

6. Pastors are encouraged to read "Initiative and Freedom," chapter 2 in William B. Oglesby, Jr.'s, *Biblical Themes for Pastoral Care* (Nashville: Abingdon Press, 1980) for a discussion on maintaining the parishioner's integrity when the pastor initiates the helping relationship.

7. Wayne E. Oates, *The Christian Pastor,* 3d ed. rev. (Philadelphia: Westminster Press, 1982), p. 79.

8. Otto A. Piper, *The Biblical View of Sex and Marriage* (New York: Charles Scribner's Sons, 1960), pp. 22, 140.

9. Charlotte H. and Howard J. Clinebell, *The Intimate Marriage,* p. 223.*

10. Paul Tillich, *Systematic Theology,* vol. 1 (Chicago: University of Chicago Press, 1951), pp. 174–186.

11. *Intimate Marriage,* p. x.

12. Tillich, vol. 1, p. 181.

13. Clifford J. Sager, *Marriage Contracts and Couple Therapy: Hidden Forces in Intimate Relationships* (New York: Brunner/Mazel, 1976), p. 3; see also pp. 10–18.

14. Tillich, vol. 1, pp. 182–186.

---

* Full facts of publication for books referred to only by author and title may be found in the back under Recommended Reading.

15. Seward Hiltner and Lowell G. Colston, *The Context of Pastoral Counseling* (Nashville: Abingdon Press, 1961), pp. 29–31.

16. The reader is referred to Martin Buber, *I and Thou* (Edinburgh: T. & T. Clark, 1937); Martin Buber, *Between Man and Man* (New York: Macmillan Co., 1965); and Reuel L. Howe, *The Miracle of Dialogue* (New York: Seabury Press, 1963).

Chapter 2: Initiating Short-term Marriage Counseling

1. Howard Clinebell, *Basic Types of Pastoral Care and Counseling,* p. 259.

2. David R. Mace, "Some Experiments with Marriage Counseling Procedures," *Family Coordinator,* vol. 22, no. 1 (January 1973), p. 29.

3. Joel S. Bergman, *Fishing for Barracuda: Pragmatics of Brief Systemic Therapy* (New York: W. W. Norton & Co., 1985), p. xv.

4. Charles W. Stewart, *The Minister as Marriage Counselor,* p. 81.

Chapter 3: Individual Sessions with Each Spouse

1. Carl R. Rogers, *Becoming Partners: Marriage and Its Alternatives* (New York: Delacorte Press, 1972), p. 206.

2. (Minneapolis) *Star Tribune,* May 15, 1987, p. 17A.

3. See Paul G. Schurman, *Money Problems and Pastoral Care* (Philadelphia: Fortress Press, 1982).

4. Sharon Wegscheider, *Another Chance: Hope and Health for the Alcoholic Family.*

5. William H. Masters, Virginia E. Johnson, and Robert C. Kolodny, *Masters and Johnson on Sex and Human Loving,* pp. 233–234.

6. Janet G. Woititz, *Adult Children of Alcoholics,* pp. 4–5.

7. Woititz, p. 103.

8. Wayne E. Oates, *The Christian Pastor,* 3d ed. rev. (Philadelphia: Westminster Press, 1982), p. 65.

Chapter 4: Concluding Joint Sessions

1. Pauline Boss, Professor of Family Social Science, University of Minnesota; (Minneapolis) *Star Tribune,* October 12, 1987, p. 4A.

2. See William B. Oglesby, Jr., *Referral in Pastoral Counseling*, rev. ed., chapter 3, "How to Refer," pp. 59–86.

Chapter 5: Special Concerns in Marriage Counseling

1. Paul Tournier, *To Understand Each Other,* John S. Gilmour, trans. (Richmond: John Knox Press, 1967), p. 38.

2. William R. Miller and Kathleen A. Jackson, *Practical Psychology for Pastors,* p. 26.

3. Carol Gilligan, *In a Different Voice: Psychological Theory and Women's Development* (Cambridge, Mass: Harvard University Press, 1982), p. 173.

4. For a discussion of the biblical theology for Christian marriage see Diana S. Richmond Garland and David E. Garland, *Beyond Companionship—Christians in Marriage.*

5. David L. Luecke, "Counseling with Couples," in *Pastoral Counseling,* Barry K. Estadt, Melvin Blanchette, John R. Compton, eds. (Englewood Cliffs, N.J.: Prentice-Hall, 1983), pp. 178–200.

6. See Charlotte H. and Howard J. Clinebell, *The Intimate Marriage,* pp. 28–34.

7. William J. Lederer and Don D. Jackson, *The Mirages of Marriage,* p. 179.

8. David Mace, *Sexual Difficulties in Marriage,* pp. 11–12.

9. Helen Singer Kaplan, *The New Sex Therapy,* pp. 121–134.

10. Male clergy are referred to Charles L. Rassieur, *The Problem Clergymen Don't Talk About.* This book discusses the male clergy's sexual response in the counseling session.

11. See Mace, *Sexual Difficulties in Marriage,* ch. 3, pp. 22–32.

12. Daniel Jay Sonkin, Del Martin, and Lenore E. A. Walker, *The Male Batterer: A Treatment Approach* (New York: Springer Publishing Co., 1985), p. 2.

13. Rita-Lou Clarke, *Pastoral Care of Battered Women,* p. 15.

14. Vicky Whipple, "Counseling Battered Women from Fundamentalist Churches," *Journal of Marital and Family Therapy,* vol. 13, no. 3 (July 1987), p. 251.

15. Carl A. Whitaker and David V. Keith, "Counseling the Dissolving Marriage," in *Counseling in Marital and Sexual Problems: A Clinician's Handbook,* 3d ed., Robert F. Stahmann and William J. Hiebert, eds. (Lexington, Mass.: D. C. Heath & Co., 1984), p. 55.

16. See William B. Oglesby, Jr., "Divorce and Remarriage in Christian Perspective," *Pastoral Psychology,* vol. 25, no. 4 (Summer 1977), pp. 282–293.

17. James L. Peterson and Nicholas Zill, "Marital Disruption, Parent-Child Relationships, and Behavior Problems in Children," *Journal of Marriage and the Family,* vol. 48 (May 1986), p. 295.

18. Andrew D. Lester, *Pastoral Care with Children in Crisis,* p. 49.

19. The pastor is also referred to *When Children Suffer: A Sourcebook for Ministry with Children in Crisis,* ed. by Andrew D. Lester, especially pp. 69–81.

20. David and Vera Mace, *In the Presence of God: Readings for Christian Marriage* (Philadelphia: Westminster Press, 1985), p. 45.

RECOMMENDED READING

Reading alone cannot be a substitute for professional supervision of one's counseling and the clinical discussion of pastoral counseling cases. However, a pastor wanting to do basic reading for pastoral marriage counseling would do well to secure these books.

Bach, George R., with Peter Wyden. *The Intimate Enemy: How to Fight Fair in Love and Marriage.* New York: William Morrow & Co., 1969; Avon Books, 1981. Basic training for couples to deal with marital conflicts.

Berne, Eric. *Games People Play: The Psychology of Human Relationships.* New York: Grove Press, 1964; Ballantine Books, 1978. The author describes the parent, adult, and child dynamics characteristic of interpersonal relationships.

Clarke, Rita-Lou. *Pastoral Care of Battered Women.* Philadelphia: Westminster Press, 1986. A basic resource for understanding abusive marriages. Includes an excellent bibliography for further reading.

Clinebell, Charlotte H. *Meet Me in the Middle: On Becoming Human Together.* New York: Harper & Row, 1973. Describes an egalitarian approach to marriage.

————, and Howard J. Clinebell. *The Intimate Marriage.* New York: Harper & Row, 1970. A sensitive and thorough discussion of the many dimensions of marital intimacy.

Clinebell, Howard J. *Basic Types of Pastoral Care and Counseling: Resources for the Ministry of Healing and Growth.* Rev. and enl. ed. Nashville: Abingdon Press, 1984. This widely used text includes a chapter on marriage enrichment and marriage crisis counseling.

————. *Growth Counseling for Marriage Enrichment: Pre-Marriage and the Early Years.* Philadelphia: Fortress Press, 1975. With this book a counselor can help couples to make need-fulfilling changes in their relationship.

————. *Growth Counseling for Mid-Years Couples.* Philadelphia: Fortress Press, 1977. Positive insights are offered for dealing with mid-life marriage problems.

Garland, Diana S. Richmond, and David E. Garland. *Beyond Companionship—Christians in Marriage.* Philadelphia: Westminster Press, 1986. A cogent presentation of a biblical theology for partnership in marriage.

Grant, Brian W. *Reclaiming the Dream: Marriage Counseling in the Parish Context.* Nashville: Abingdon Press, 1986. An experienced counselor discusses the technical aspects of marriage counseling.

Hulme, William E. *Pastoral Care and Counseling: Using the Unique Resources of the Christian Tradition.* Minneapolis: Augsburg Publishing House, 1981. The author shows how faith resources can be integrated into the counseling process.

Kaplan, Helen Singer. *The New Sex Therapy: Active Treatment of Sexual Dysfunctions.* New York: Brunner/Mazel, 1974. This book will help the pastor to understand the dynamics of serious marital sexual problems.

Lederer, William J., and Don D. Jackson. *The Mirages of Marriage.* New York: W. W. Norton & Co., 1968. A standard work that examines basic assumptions and misunderstandings about marriage.

Lester, Andrew D. *Pastoral Care with Children in Crisis.* Philadelphia: Westminster Press, 1985. An essential guide for pastors concerned about the children of conflicted marriages.

————, ed. *When Children Suffer: A Sourcebook for Ministry with Children in Crisis.* Philadelphia: Westminster Press, 1987. Especially important is Benjamin T. Griffin's chapter, "Children Whose Parents Are Divorcing."

Mace, David. *Love and Anger in Marriage.* Grand Rapids: Zondervan Publishing House, 1982. A recognized authority on marriage and marriage counseling discusses anger in the context of growth in all dimensions of the marriage.

————. *Sexual Difficulties in Marriage.* Philadelphia: Fortress Press, 1972. The author offers his views on sexuality in marriage.

————, and Vera Mace. *How to Have a Happy Marriage.* Nashville: Abingdon Press, 1977, 1983. Offering a step-by-step plan for marriage growth and enrichment, this is a book pastors can recommend for use by parishioners.

Masters, William H., and Virginia E. Johnson. *Human Sexual Inadequacy.* Boston: Little, Brown, & Co., 1970. One of the standard resources for helping a pastor to understand sexual problems in marriage.

————, ————, and Robert C. Kolodny. *Masters and Johnson on Sex and Human Loving.* Boston: Little, Brown & Co., 1986. An authoritative resource that goes beyond biology to examine the wider aspects of sexual intimacy and communication.

Miller, Sherod, Daniel Wackman, Elam Nunnally, and Carol Saline. *Straight Talk: A New Way to Get Closer to Others by Saying What You Really Mean.* New York: Rawson, Wade Publishers, 1981. Based on the famous Couple Communication Program, the book explains how to share deep feelings without attacking or blaming one's mate.

Miller, William R., and Kathleen A. Jackson. *Practical Psychology for Pastors.* Englewood Cliffs, N.J.: Prentice-Hall, 1985. Basic principles of counseling psychology are outlined for the pastoral counselor, including a chapter on relationship counseling.

Monfalcone, Wesley R. *Coping with Abuse in the Family.* Philadelphia: Westminster Press, 1980. Family abuse and spouse abuse are examined, with practical steps outlined for dealing with destructive and violent behavior.

Oglesby, William B., Jr. *Referral in Pastoral Counseling.* Rev. ed. Nashville: Abingdon Press, 1978. This important resource discusses all aspects of referral for the parish pastor.

Rassieur, Charles L. *The Problem Clergymen Don't Talk About.* Philadelphia: Westminster Press, 1976. Help is offered to male clergy for understanding and dealing with their own sexual feelings evoked in the counseling process.

Rice, F. Philip. *Sexual Problems in Marriage: Help from a Christian Counselor.* Philadelphia: Westminster Press, 1978. The writer provides a thorough and readable discussion of sexual difficulties and their treatment.

Rubin, Lillian B. *Intimate Strangers: Men and Women Together.* New York: Harper & Row, 1983. This book addresses the struggles men and women have as they work together for intimacy, companionship, sharing, communication, and equality.

Shelp, Earl E., and Ronald H. Sunderland. *AIDS and the Church.* Philadelphia: Westminster Press, 1987. An insightful discussion that will help the pastor to make informed counseling responses.

Stewart, Charles W. *The Minister as Marriage Counselor.* Rev. ed. Nashville: Abingdon Press, 1970. A basic text on the essential themes of pastoral marriage counseling.

Sunderland, Ronald H., and Earl E. Shelp. *AIDS, A Manual for Pastoral Care.* Philadelphia: Westminster Press, 1987. Will assist the pastor in caring for those with AIDS and their families and associates.

Visher, Emily B., and John S. Visher. *Stepfamilies: A Guide to Working with Stepparents and Stepchildren.* New York: Brunner/Mazel, 1979. Required reading for pastors and for spouses in stepfamilies.

Wegscheider, Sharon. *Another Chance: Hope and Health for the Alcoholic Family.* Palo Alto, Calif.: Science & Behavior Books, 1981. The dynamics and roles that typically occur in alcoholic marriage and family systems are explained for ready recognition by the counselor.

Woititz, Janet Geringer. *Adult Children of Alcoholics.* Hollywood, Fla.: Health Communications, 1983. An informative introduction to the problems characteristic of thousands of persons from alcoholic homes.

Pastors are also encouraged to refer to the following journals:
Journal of Marital and Family Therapy
Journal of Marriage and the Family
Journal of Pastoral Care
Journal of Pastoral Psychotherapy
Pastoral Psychology